First World War
and Army of Occupation
War Diary
France, Belgium and Germany

16 DIVISION
Headquarters, Branches and Services
Royal Army Veterinary Corps
Assistant Director Veterinary Services
18 December 1915 - 28 February 1919

WO95/1961/3

The Naval & Military Press Ltd
www.nmarchive.com
Published in association with The National Archives

Published by

The Naval & Military Press Ltd

Unit 10 Ridgewood Industrial Park,

Uckfield, East Sussex,

TN22 5QE England

Tel: +44 (0) 1825 749494

www.naval-military-press.com

www.nmarchive.com

This diary has been reprinted in facsimile from the original. Any imperfections are inevitably reproduced and the quality may fall short of modern type and cartographic standards.

© **Crown Copyright**
Images reproduced by permission of The National Archives, London, England, 2015.

Contents

Document type	Place/Title	Date From	Date To
Heading	WO95/1961. 16 Division Headquarters Branches & Services Dec 1915-Feb 1919 Assistant Director Veterinary Services.		
Heading	D.A.D.O.S. 16th Div.		
Heading	A.D.V.S. 16th Div. Vol I Dec 15 Feb 19		
War Diary	Farnborough S.W.	18/12/1915	18/12/1915
War Diary	S'Hampton	18/12/1915	18/12/1915
War Diary	Havre	19/12/1915	19/12/1915
War Diary	Chocques	20/12/1915	20/12/1915
War Diary	Drouvin	21/12/1915	31/12/1915
Heading	A.D.I.S. 16th Div. Vol. 2 Jan		
War Diary	Drouvin Bomy.	01/01/1916	08/01/1916
War Diary	Bomy. Amettes	08/01/1916	12/01/1916
War Diary	Amettes	13/01/1916	31/01/1916
Heading	A.D.V.S. 16. Div. Vol. 3.		
War Diary	Amettes	01/02/1916	27/02/1916
War Diary	Busnes	27/02/1916	29/02/1916
Heading	A.D.V.S. 16th Div Vol. 4		
War Diary	Busnes.	01/03/1916	09/03/1916
War Diary	Lillers	09/03/1916	27/03/1916
War Diary	Noeux-Les-Mines.	27/03/1916	19/04/1916
Miscellaneous	The D.A.G. 3rd Echelon	03/06/1916	03/06/1916
War Diary	Noeux-Les-Mines.	01/05/1916	31/05/1916
Miscellaneous	The D.A.G. 3rd Echelon	01/07/1916	01/07/1916
War Diary	Noeux-Les-Mines	01/06/1916	30/07/1916
Heading	War Diary. A.D.V.S. 16th Division. Month Of August, 1916. Volume:- 9		
War Diary	Noeux-Les-Mines.	06/08/1916	26/08/1916
War Diary	Raimbert	26/08/1916	28/08/1916
War Diary	Chocques	29/08/1916	29/08/1916
War Diary	Longeau. Corbie.	30/08/1916	31/08/1916
War Diary	F. 2. b. (Albert Combined Sheet)	31/08/1916	31/08/1916
Heading	War Diary A.D.V.S. 16th Division For Month Of September, 1916. Volume 10		
War Diary	Fork Tree. (albert L.2b.0.9.)	01/09/1916	04/09/1916
War Diary	Fork. Tree.	04/09/1916	04/09/1916
War Diary	Citadel (F21.b.)	05/09/1916	09/09/1916
War Diary	Citadel.	09/09/1916	11/09/1916
War Diary	Corbie	11/09/1916	18/09/1916
War Diary	Hallen-Court.	18/09/1916	21/09/1916
War Diary	Bailleul	21/09/1916	21/09/1916
War Diary	Westoutre (Belgium Sheet 28. S.W. M.G.C.)	21/09/1916	23/09/1916
War Diary	Westoutre	24/09/1916	30/09/1916
Heading	War Diary Month Of October, 1916. Volume 11 A.D.V.S. 16th. Division		
War Diary	Westoutre	05/10/1916	31/10/1916
Heading	War Diary. For Month Of November, 1916. Volume 12. A.D.V.S. 16th Division		
War Diary	Westoutre.	01/11/1916	30/11/1916

Heading	War Diary For Month Of December, 1916. Volume 13. A.D.V.S. 16th Division		
War Diary	Westoutre	01/12/1916	31/12/1916
Heading	War Diary for month of January, 1917. Volume 14 A.D.V.S. 16th Division		
War Diary	Westoutre	08/01/1917	31/01/1917
Heading	War Diary. For Month Of February, 1917. Volume 15 Unit- A.D.V.S. 16th Division		
War Diary	Westoutre	01/02/1917	28/02/1917
Heading	War Diary For Month Of March, 1917. Volume 16 Unit- A.D.V.S. 16th Division		
War Diary	Westoutre	01/03/1917	06/03/1917
Heading	War Diary For Month Of April, 1917. Volume 17 Unit- A.D.V.S. 16th Division		
War Diary	Locre M 29b.3.9 (France Sheet 28. S.W.)	01/04/1917	06/04/1917
War Diary	Locre	07/04/1917	31/05/1917
Heading	War Diary. For Month Of June, 1917. Volume 19 Unit- D.A.D.V.S. 16th Division		
War Diary	Locre	01/06/1917	13/06/1917
War Diary	Merris	13/06/1917	17/06/1917
War Diary	Locre.	17/06/1917	18/06/1917
War Diary	Merris.	18/06/1917	20/06/1917
War Diary	Godewaersvelde	20/06/1917	22/06/1917
War Diary	Zeggers-Cappel	22/06/1917	23/06/1917
Heading	War Diary. For Month Of July, 1917. Volume 20 Unit- D.A.D.V.S. 16 Division		
War Diary	Zeggers-Cappel	01/07/1916	23/07/1916
War Diary	Poperinghe	24/07/1917	31/07/1917
Heading	War Diary. For Month Of August, 1917. Volume 21 Unit D.A.D.V.S. 16 Division		
War Diary	Poperinghe	01/08/1917	03/08/1917
War Diary	Brandhoek Camp.	04/08/1917	17/08/1917
War Diary	Watou	18/08/1917	21/08/1917
War Diary	Achiet Le Petit	27/08/1917	28/08/1917
Heading	War Diary. For Month Of August, 1917. Volume 22 Unit D.A.D.V.S. 16th Division		
War Diary	Moyenneville	01/09/1917	18/09/1917
War Diary	Behagnies	26/09/1917	30/09/1917
Heading	War Diary For Month Of October, 1917. Unit D.A.D.V.S. 16 Division Volume Number 23		
War Diary	Behagnies	01/10/1917	31/10/1917
Heading	War Diary For Month Of November, 1917. Volume 24 Unit- D.A.D.V.S. 16 Division		
War Diary	Behagnies	01/11/1917	30/11/1917
Heading	War Diary For Month Of December, 1917. Volume 25 Unit- D.A.D.V.S. 16th Division		
War Diary	Behagnies	01/12/1917	02/12/1917
War Diary	Ypres	03/12/1917	04/12/1917
War Diary	Flamicourt	05/12/1917	06/12/1917
War Diary	Villers Faucon	07/12/1917	17/12/1917
Heading	War Diary. For Month Of January, 1918. Volume 26. Unit- D.A.D.V.S. 16 Division		
War Diary	Villers Faucon	01/01/1918	21/01/1918
War Diary	Tincourt.	22/01/1918	21/03/1918
War Diary	Doingt	22/03/1918	22/03/1918
War Diary	Biaches Cappy	23/03/1918	24/03/1918

War Diary	Morlancourt	25/03/1918	25/03/1918
War Diary	La Motte	26/03/1918	26/03/1918
War Diary	Petit Blangy	27/03/1918	31/03/1918
War Diary	Fauquembergues	11/04/1918	15/04/1918
War Diary	Aire	16/04/1918	15/05/1918
War Diary	Samer	16/05/1918	16/06/1918
War Diary	Boulogne	17/06/1918	18/06/1918
War Diary	Aldershot	19/06/1918	27/06/1918
War Diary	Bourley Camp Aldershot	28/06/1918	30/06/1918
War Diary	Samer.	01/08/1918	18/08/1918
War Diary	Monchy Cayeux.	19/08/1918	22/08/1918
War Diary	Ruitz	23/08/1918	22/09/1918
War Diary	Drouvin	01/10/1918	06/10/1918
War Diary	Sailly Labourse	07/10/1918	17/10/1918
War Diary	Billy Berclau	18/10/1918	19/10/1918
War Diary	Plalempin.	20/10/1918	21/10/1918
War Diary	Templeuve	22/10/1918	10/11/1918
War Diary	Taintignies	11/11/1918	16/11/1918
War Diary	Attiches	17/11/1918	17/11/1918
War Diary	Avelin	07/12/1918	28/02/1919

was/1861
16 Division
Headquarters Branches of
Services

Dec 1915 - Feb 1919

ASSISTANT DIRECTOR VETERINARY
SERVICES.

(6)

b A D O.
16 t Dic:
———————

A.S.W. 16th Div.
Vol I

12/7931

Dec '18
Feb '19

Army Form C. 2118

A.D. ? ? 16th Div ? ?

WAR DIARY
or
INTELLIGENCE SUMMARY.
(Erase heading not required.)

Instructions regarding War Diaries and Intelligence Summaries are contained in F. S. Regs., Part II. and the Staff Manual respectively. Title pages will be prepared in manuscript.

Place	Date	Hour	Summary of Events and Information	Remarks and references to Appendices
FARN-BOROUGH S.W.	18.12.15	10 am	Lieut. LENTON. A.V.C. entrained with 47. M.V.S.	J.O.A.
"	"	3 pm	Lieut. BROAD A.V.C. entrained with H.Q. 16th Div. Train	
"	"	4.30 pm	entrained with H.Q. 16th Div.?	
S'HAMPTON.	"	6 pm	Detrain & embark S.S. MAIDAN. - 62 Lowes H.Q. Coy. Train & 65 H.P. Bar.?	J.O.A.
"	"	5.30 pm	Sail	
HAVRE	19.12.15	7 am	Arrive & proceed to Disembark.	J.O.A.
"	"	11 am	Proceed by road to No 5 - Rest Camp. Remain there the day	
"	"	9.30 pm	Entrain POINT I	
"	"	10.30 pm	Leave HAVRE	
CHOCQUES	20.12.15	8 pm	Arrive, Detrain, proceeding by car to DROUVIN, going into billets.	J.O.A.
DROUVIN	21.12.15		Top. L. ? ? M.V.S. & ? ? & canvas.	
"	"	9 am	Visit S.D. Horse. LABUISSIERE.	J.O.A.
"	22.12.15	am	Visited to at HESDIGNEUL, HOUCHIN, VERQUIN, & VAUDRICOURT.	J.O.A.
"	"	pm	NOEUX-LES-MINES.	
"	23.12.15	am	NOEUX-LES-MINES. MAZINGARBE, PHILOSOPHE, etc.	J.O.A.
"	"		In this area forwarded sick to 1st Divisional M.V.S.	
"	"	pm	Two sent to billet M.V.S. at GOSNAY. Drew 4? ? J.O.A.	
"	"		to move when tomorrow	
"	24.12.15	am	47. M.V.S. move to GOSNAY. MAP 36 D30 & A. obtain ? of stables & hay which they subsequently ?	J.O.A.
"	"		Visit S.D. Horse LABUISSIERE.	

2353   Wt. W2544/1454 700,000 5/15 D. D. & L. A.D.S.S./Forms/C. 2118.

WAR DIARY or INTELLIGENCE SUMMARY

Army Form C. 2118

A.D.V.S. 16 H Div.

Place	Date	Hour	Summary of Events and Information	Remarks and references to Appendices
DROUVIN.	25/12/15	a.m.	54 + 64 + Anglian Artillery Ln. arrangements by the Divisional Vet Officer units (4 Brig Gen + DAC) at ECCEDECQUES, LIERES, LESPESSES, AMES, & FAUCHENHEM. – A.V.C. Army offices notify	
"	26/12/15		bath twenty. Vet Hosp ? D.D.V.S. of Army at HOUCHIN & HESDIGNEUL	
"	27/12/15		Inspected 2 E Cart Anglian Artillery. Sick horses are to come from evans to 10/15 H Div 1 Fv V.S. at LILLERS.	off
"	28/12/15	a.m.	Visit units to 4 HESDIGNEUL, GOSNAY, HOUCHIN	off
"	29/12/15	a.m.	8 DUBLIN Fug + 9 MUNSTER Fus. transferred NEDON, & NEDONCHELLE Visit units to at VERQUIN & NOEUX-LES-MINES.	off
"	30/12/15	a.m.	S.J. HORSE mvs. to WESTREHEM 6 Dublin Fus. moved from HOUCHIN to NOEUX-LES-MINES. 7 L'ton Fus. 8 E. Surrey Fus. & R.Dio L.Reg.F. move to vicinity of AMETTES, in units to for LAIRES, BEAUMETZ, + BOMY. to AUCHY-AU-BOIS, to find sick for MVS. In true to O.C.4 ? H.V. Ey MAR 36 A. 7/3 cl.	off
"	31/12/15	a.m.	sand advance party to AUCHY-AU-BOIS tomorrow	off
			visit units in vicinity of GOSNAY.	
		p.m.	AUCHY-AU-BOIS & WESTREHEM.	

Whils at DROUVIN, officers A.V.C. and sub billets as follow :–

LIEUT HOWE – HOUCHIN,
BROAD – HESDIGNEUL
LENTON (O.C. MVS) GOSNAY.

MS.S. 16th Sér.
Vol: 2

Jan

Army Form C. 2118.

WAR DIARY
or
INTELLIGENCE SUMMARY.

(Erase heading not required.)

A.D.V.S. 16th Division

Instructions regarding War Diaries and Intelligence Summaries are contained in F.S. Regs., Part II. and the Staff Manual respectively. Title pages will be prepared in manuscript.

Place	Date	Hour	Summary of Events and Information	Remarks and references to Appendices
DROUVIN	1.1.16	9 am	Leave with H.Q. the Division. 7 horses evacuated by M.V.S. (47 M.V.S. now £36.A.T.13d.)	
BOMY.		11 am	Arrive " "	
		12.30 pm	Visit troops at AMETTES & AUCHY-AU-BOIS.	
	2.1.16		Visit troops at NEDON & AUCHY.	J.O.H.
	3.1.16	am	Report to D.D.V.S. AIRE.	J.O.H.
	4.1.16		Inspect horses of 1/1st, 1/2nd, 4/1, 3rd B.Sec. & D.A.C. of London Gun(?) Artillery. Condition excellent, shoeing fair.	J.O.H.
	5.1.16		Visit VIELERS with D.A.D.O.S., arrange for interment of sick animals from 47 M.V.S., FOUQUEREUIL being near dead. and distance too far.	J.O.H.
	6.1.16		Visit troops at SENLIS, HEZECQUES & BERQUINGHEM.	J.O.H.
	7.1.16		95 horses evacuated by M.V.S.	J.O.H.
	8.1.16		27 " " " " " Conducting party supplied by M.V.S.	J.O.H.
			1st Div. M.V.S.	J.O.H.
BOMY.		9 am	Leave with H.Q. the Division	
LAMETTES		9.30 am	Arrive " "	
	10.1.16	am	Visit AUCHY & LIERES.	
		pm	Inspect 4 1/3rd London Regt R.F.A	
		pm	to AIRE, report to D.D.V.S.	J.O.H.
	11.1.16	am	Visit troops NEDON & AMES	
		pm	Report to D.D.V.S. AIRE.	J.O.H.
	12.1.16	am	Inspect horses of 7th Rg L. Irish Rifles. Condition Exc? at Lumbres Reg? & 8th Leinsters Geo.	
		pm	42 horses evacuated by 47 M.V.S.	J.O.H.

Army Form C. 2118.

Instructions regarding War Diaries and Intelligence Summaries are contained in F. S. Regs., Part II. and the Staff Manual respectively. Title pages will be prepared in manuscript.

A.D.V.S. 16th Div.

WAR DIARY
or
INTELLIGENCE SUMMARY.
(Erase heading not required.)

Place	Date	Hour	Summary of Events and Information	Remarks and references to Appendices
BAMETTES	13.1.16		LIEUT. HOWE A.V.C. granted special leave to proceed to England.	DDA
	14.1.16		Inspect 7th Irish Rifles, 9th Dublins, & 8nl Signal Coy R.E.	DDA
	15.1.16		1 section of 10 D.A.C. — Inspected with unit.	DDA
			2 sections (6) Coy R.E.	
	16.1.16		16 Animals evacuated to By 47 M.V.S.	
			Sergt. LAVINGTON A.V.C. attached 48th Infy. Bde - sick - sent to 112? Fd. Ambulance. Temporarily replaced by Pte. FURLONGER A.V.C.	DDA
			Visit troops at HESDIGNEUL & LES BREBIS.	
	17.1.16		Inspects 8th Dublins & 9th Munsters.	DDA
			40 Animals evacuated to By 47 M.V.S.	DDA
	18.1.16		Visit troops at PHILOSOPHE, MAZINGARBE, LES BREBIS, HESDIGNEUL.	DDA
	19.1.16		Inspect South Irish Horse, C. Squadron	
			Veterinary stores and Cavalry Depôts at Rifle pound.	DDA
	20.1.16		Inspect 8th Dublins, 7th Regt Irish Rifles & Signal Coy.	DDA
	21.1.16		65 Remounts arrive for Division.	DDA
	22.1.16		Inspect 1/3rd B'gn R.F.A. & M.M.P.	DDA
	23.1.16		Lieut. HOWE A.V.C. returns from leave.	DDA
			Start holding enquiries of horses with mange-found palpebral itch. All V.Os. instructed to look for dd in B'gd A	DDA
			at army.	

Army Form C. 2118.

WAR DIARY
or
INTELLIGENCE SUMMARY. A.D-V.S. 16th Div[n]
(Erase heading not required.)

Instructions regarding War Diaries and Intelligence Summaries are contained in F.S. Regs., Part II and the Staff Manual respectively. Title pages will be prepared in manuscript.

Place	Date	Hour	Summary of Events and Information	Remarks and references to Appendices
AMETTES	24.1.16		Inspect D.A.C. & H.Q.R.A. 3. G.S. wagons arriving from whom trouble will be known in route for ABBEVILLE, to exchange for floats (lorry)	J.O.A.
	25.1.16	8.15am	37 animals went fwd from 4) tribes. Inspect 4 G.S. wagons before leaving M.V.S. for ABBEVILLE. Inspect animals at HESDIGNEUL. NOEUX-LES-MINES & MAZINGARBE.	J.O.A.
	26.1.16		Inspect South Irish Horse, 1st R.F.L. sick R.F.L.s, 8th Dublins, 11th Bde R.S.a. rides/vers/g to B.Sn at LIERES.	J.O.A.
	27.1.16		Inspecting lines of communications animals while in transit.	J.O.A.
	28.1.16		also inspect the P.48th Inf. Bde, 7th Leinsters, & 6th Ryl Dublin. Ryl. weekly visits from front line.	J.O.A.
	29.1.16		Inspecting transport animals Cs. 26 animals evacuated by M.V.S.	J.O.A.
	30.1.16		Inspect reports for forage with review to purchase.	J.O.A.
	31.1.16		Inspecting trenches animals Cs.	J.O.A.

WAR DIARY
INTELLIGENCE SUMMARY.
(Erase heading not required.)

Army Form C. 2118.

A Sqn 1/1 ? Bde ?

Owing to the Divisions being very scattered, & owing to the Bde being attached to other Divisions, it has been most difficult to make satisfactory veterinary arrangements. Lieut. HOWE is at present attached to 4/1 H. & is the Sn. no. 2 his duties now with 2 Officers (including O.C. Sqn.) for troops in back billets, & the infantry transport requires continual supervision, their knowledge of stable management & feeding being very limited, & the material (personnel) inferior.

Hay ration has been reduced to 6 lbs & hay which is being supplemented by :—

6 lbs straw (or 3 lbs ensuro grain, or 1 lb ensuro cake, the latter equivalent being impossible) and 2 lbs bulrush or mango ??. Great difficulty however in getting these from Chier Supervisor

[signature]

A.D.V.S.
16. Div.
Vol. 3.

WAR DIARY or INTELLIGENCE SUMMARY

Army Form C. 2118.

A.D.V.S. 16th Division

Place	Date	Hour	Summary of Events and Information	Remarks and references to Appendices
AMETTES	1.2.16	am	Visited troops at LESPESSES, TAUCHY-AU-BOIS. Horses of East Anglian Artillery showing 5th V.S. a "smart appearance" prior to their march to villain. Pantings - typical frost.	
		pm	Inspect 9th Sub Dist two.	B
	2.2.16	10.30 am	Inspect 1/1st Bde London Artillery.	
		4 pm	Inspected 99 Remounts for 8th St QUILLERS. Show.	for J.H
	3.2.16	am	Inspected 1/1st WILSHAW M.V.C. joined 47th Inf Bde relieving Bde Hd 122 D.V.S. JQSH for J.H	
		pm	8/Surg. WILSHAW M.V.C. joined 47th Inf Bde relieving Bde Hd 122 D.V.S. who has reverted to permanent post.	
	4.2.16	am	Inspect 8 & 4 Dublin two	JQSH for J.H
		pm	Inspect following units of this Division, attached to 47 & 15th Division - 1/7th Royal Dublin Rifles, 1st Connaught Rangers, 11th Hamps Bye, 9th Dublin two, 9th Hampster two, 143 Coy A.S.C.	JQSH
	5.2.16		Saw 8 & 4 Dublin two and the march.	
	6.2.16	am	Inspected surface inspection everywhere a farm at MARTIN JOSEPH, MONTCORNET. Diagnosis mange, though not confirmed microscopically.	JQSH for J.H
		pm	Reports two came to Hd Q of the Division.	
	7.2.16	am	Visited troops under in campment of BUSNES, ENGUINE GAHEN, WESTREHEM. AUCHY-AU-BOIS.	JQSH
		pm	Visited troops at WESTREHEM. AUCHY-AU-BOIS	A considerable number of mange points.

Army Form C. 2118.

WAR DIARY
or
INTELLIGENCE SUMMARY.
(Erase heading not required.)

A.D.V.S.
18th Div"

Instructions regarding War Diaries and Intelligence Summaries are contained in F. S. Regs. Part II. and the Staff Manual respectively. Title pages will be prepared in manuscript.

Place	Date	Hour	Summary of Events and Information	Remarks and references to Appendices
AMETTES	8.2.16	10 am	Inspect 112th & 40th Ambulance	JOH
		3 pm	8th Tunnrs Cie two.	
	9.2.16		Visit CANTRAINNES forelect establishts for ZnVS	JOH
	10.2.16	10 am	D.Dv.S. 1st Army visited to D.A.C. (10th)	
			Quick turn purchases locally for manufacture a	JOH
			Hig Calais Siciphdown	
	11.2.16	am	Visits troops at Billery + AMG8.	JOH
	12.2.16		Inspect 6th Conn. Raijs. 9th Tunnrs 7th & 48th Sap. 138th JOH	JOH
	14.2.16	am	Report to D.D.V.S. 1st army at AIRES.	JOH
	15.2.16	am	Inspect Hd Dublins 9th HR aust Visit troops ar VIGNY	JOH
			RELY.	
	16.2.16	10 am	Inspect 9th Dublin two.	JOH
		2.30pm	Inspect skin cases of 10th D.A.C. by Colonel Chief men returning unfit Turning , mange, purrious	JOH
			at M.V.S.	
	17.2.16		Examine dogs & Jorehoufs from horse at MONT CORNET	
			finds ACARUS SATC.O.T.S. send acertipat D.D.V.S. the Ovg JOH	
	18.2.16	am	Inspect 11th Hampshire Ryfr.	JOH
	19.2.16	am	15th CO F.R. 9 156 Cty R.	

Army Form C. 2118.

WAR DIARY
or
INTELLIGENCE SUMMARY.

A.D.V.S.
16th Divn

(Erase heading not required.)

Instructions regarding War Diaries and Intelligence Summaries are contained in F.S. Regs., Part II. and the Staff Manual respectively. Title pages will be prepared in manuscript.

Place	Date	Hour	Summary of Events and Information	Remarks and references to Appendices
AMETTES	20.2.16	10 am	Inspect sick & proposed emptying of 1/3 Bde. R.F.A.	JDA
		2 pm	Inspect Remounts at PELLERS station.	
	21.2.16	10.30 am	9th Hussars two.	
		11.30 am	8th Dublin two.	
			16th Divl Artillery bar received orders — 77th (How), 177th, 180th & 182nd Bdes R.F.A. also Div.e. Tpt.	
			49th Inf Bde. Inspect 180th Bde. — BLESSY, near 182nd Bde. with ERNESSE	JDA
	22.2.16	10.30 am	6th Connaught Regt.	
		11.30 am	7th Ryl. Irish Regt.	
		6 pm	Visit H.Q. London Artillery Bourecq — relieving 1/4th Bde. R.F.A. Tomorrow.	JDA
	23.2.16		1/4 Bde. relieved — in the Divnal prepared tent.	
			1/4 Bde. welcomed.	JDA
		11 am	Inspect 7th Leinsters two.	
	24.2.16	10 am	Visit H.Q. 49 Inf. Bde. & 7th Irish Fus. — entrainment.	JDA
			Inspect 6th Ryl. Irish two.	
		pm	Visit 8th Lincs two.	
	25.2.16	am	Inspect 9th Lancs two.	JDA
	26.2.16	am	Visit & inspect FONTAINE-LES-HERMANS, NEDON etc.	JDA

WAR DIARY
or
INTELLIGENCE SUMMARY.

Army Form C. 2118.

Place	Date	Hour	Summary of Events and Information	Remarks and references to Appendices
AMETTES	27.2.16	9am	Left with HQrs 9th the Div to arrive.	J.A.
BUSNES		9.30am	Unable to find suitable billets pwtawaiting orders to remain at VCHY-AU-BOIS, unable further orders 47 Div. V.S. prior to LA PIERRIERE inspects, & visits from 2/1/34 Fd Ambulance.	J.A.
	29.2.16		Owing to have weather, roads very bad, however from Feb 22nd to 28th 49 Fd Amb & 3 St Thorpes no front cars with them over seas, & are experience had great difficulty in moving their transport.	J.A.

WAR DIARY
INTELLIGENCE SUMMARY
(Erase heading not required.)

Army Form C. 2118

Place	Date	Hour	Summary of Events and Information	Remarks and references to Appendices
BUSNES	29.2.16	6pm	Office has moved from AMETTES to RELY. This made Ordnance and easier storage accommodation very bad - in barns with straw and manure - they are cleared as far as possible. The Division moved into 10C Café Recreo Area on 28th and Ross's Office has moved last day at BUSNES. The kit store and office have found new 36. A. P. 26. a. The 49 Infantry Brigade and Divisional Artillery have now joined the Division and winter clothing has been issued. Demands for boots have not been so heavy owing to last built- possibly because material for the repair of boots has been coming through regularly in advance to demands - It has been decided to establish a Divisional Ammunition Dump as soon as the Division has settled down in a locality where proper facilities in the way of a building can be obtained.	

J.S. Oxford
Lieut.
DADOS 16th Divn.

ADVS
16th Dec
Vol. 4

WAR DIARY or INTELLIGENCE SUMMARY

Army Form C. 2118.

A.D.V.S.
16th Division

Place	Date	Hour	Summary of Events and Information	Remarks and references to Appendices
BUSNES	1.3.16	9 am	By car to visit AMETTES, BLESSY & WITTERNESSE, in area just vacated, & to enquire if any horses belonging to units of this Division have been abandoned, & into the rumours about mules (all previous reports). Two forwarded on by road & taken into Depôt. Call at AUCHY-AU-BOIS to see detachment of Mr. V.S. left behind with 4 "bad" cases. These ordered to proceed to 47th London Div. A.V.S. at LILLERS tomorrow.	
		2 pm	To GUARBECQ, BERGUETTE & MAXINGHEM, to visit artillery brigades.	
	2.3.16	10.30 am	H.Q. R.F.A. — GUARBECQ. — Conditions fair, small boy Infant (?) H.Q. R.F.A. — GUARBECQ. — two horses sent a few days ago to 47th. V.S. at LA PIERRIERE.	
		2.30 pm	Visit Mr. V.S.	
		5 pm	Attend conference at H.Q. Div.	
			No. 6940 Serj. T. WILSHAW A.V.C. attached to H.Q. 47 Div. Bde was recently transferred by F.G.C.M. finding, & this man was recently transferred from 34½ Div when in charge of No. 28464 Serj. F. HILL A.V.C. Evidence to have, on reverse, to permanent rank.	
			4) Mr. V.S. evacuated 8 cases. Mallein of animals. 16th Div. Artillery by order. Issued of antidote to Infanterie.	

Army Form C. 2118.

WAR DIARY
or
INTELLIGENCE SUMMARY.

A.D.V.S. 16th Division

(Erase heading not required.)

Place	Date	Hour	Summary of Events and Information	Remarks and references to Appendices
BUSNES	3.3.16	10.30 am	Inspected 77th Bde R.F.A. at BERGUETTE - Condition of horses seen afew to the V.S. The majority of the horses are standing in the open - country so water-logged in the region of the CANAL, notwithstanding the Brick floors laid, horses knee deep in places, one a serious fracture of cannon with evidence over they - so far no trans-time-proof covers are also being supplied by the R.E. J.O.H.	
		2.30 pm	Conference of veterinary officers at my office.	
		6 pm	Interviewing A.D.V.S. 47th London Division officer in view to taking over the billets at present occupied by this M.V.S. if this Division moves into station.	
	4.3.16 am	Visited troops in vicinity of LA PIERRIERE & LAMIQUELLERIE.	
			4) M.V.S. evacuated 22 animals returning abt 17 LS.S. Report to D.D.V.S. 1st Army that the 47th Sup f. MINCHINGTON A.C. + 10796. Sup f. PODD A.V.C. attached 180 (at 4)) MBSD. J.O.H.	
	5.3.16 am	Sup f. PODD A.V.C. having been reported sick, respectfully been examined and sent to 1/1 FD.AMBULANCE. Visited troops at HAM-EN-ARTOIS, + BOUREC Q, inspected proposed Cantons of 1/1 FD.AMBULANCE. J.O.H.	

Army Form C. 2118.

WAR DIARY
or
INTELLIGENCE SUMMARY.
(Erase heading not required.)

A.D.V.S.
16th Division

(3)

Place	Date	Hour	Summary of Events and Information	Remarks and references to Appendices
BUSNES	6.3.16	10 am	Inspected 182nd Bde. R.F.A. at MAZINGHAM - condition good; shoeing fair.	J.O.A.
	7.3.16		4) m.v.S. evacuated 21 animals, entraining LILLERS	
		9.30 am	Visited R.A.H.Q. or - BERGUETTE, interviewed vet officers of 177th & 180th Bdes; inspected horses of 180th Bde. which have been recently invalided.	
		2.30 pm	Visited 'C' Squadron. S.I. Horse. CANTRAINNES, & new ow to LILLERS horses at Div. S. 4) London Bn.	J.O.A.
	8.3.16	9.30 am	To LILLERS, to arrange billets for 4) m.v.S. here in officers arrange billets for men, & horses are to billets later.	J.O.A.
		pm	4) m.v.S. evacuated 16 horses, entraining LILLERS.	
	9.3.16	9.30 am	To COTTES to reconnoitre home left behind by H.Q. 4) m.v.S. Two animals unable to walk on to LILLERS.	J.O.A.
		1.30 pm	Leave.	
LILLERS		2 pm	Arrive. H.) m.v.S. evacuating 3 men & four in to billet & evacuating this morning by London m.v.S. Small fatigue left behind at LA BIERIERE, with party of two men there will be received tomorrow. Notification received from H.Q. 4) Inf. Bde. that A.O. 63240 Sergt. Wildhaus A.V.C has been attached by F.C.M. for sentence to the Labour Co. 21st July to Punishment No. I	J.O.A.

WAR DIARY or INTELLIGENCE SUMMARY

Army Form C. 2118.

A.D.V.S. 16th Division

Place	Date	Hour	Summary of Events and Information	Remarks and references to Appendices
LILLERS	10.3.16	pm	Conference of Veterinary Officers. Partial re-distribution with 16th D.V.S. & D.D.V.S. visit to V.S.	J.O.T.
	11.3.16	9.30am	Inspect H.Q. 48th Inf. Bde, 7th R. Innisk. Fus, 7th R.D. Fus, 9th Innisks, & 8th Dub. Fus. Great improvement in conditions for stabling.	J.O.T.
		2pm	Visited 157th Bde R.F.A. & 16th D.A.C. all satisfactory. One very bad case Strangles 47th M.V.S. evacuate 7 animals.	J.O.T.
	12.3.16	7.30am	Visit 182nd Bde R.F.A. – BELLERY	
		10.30am	Inspect H.Q. 47th Inf. Bde, 7th Leinsters & 8th Munsters at ALLOUAGNE, & BAS RIEUX	J.O.T.
	13.3.16	10am	Inspect 143 & 144 Coy A.S.C. – RAIMBERT. Inspect 3 reported doubtful cases to mallein of 182 Bde R.F.A. – BELLERY. Consider not suspicious, but gave work subcutaneous injection.	J.O.T.
	14.3.16	8.30am	Visit ADVS 15th Div at NOEUX-LES-MINES, to arrange re taking over the V.S. billet when this Div moves to forward area.	
		3pm	Inspect 18 remounts on their arrival LILLERS station. I.D. unknown condition.	
		4pm	47 M.V.S. evacuate 15 animals, entraining LILLERS station. Case suspected mange reports from 182 Bde R.F.A. – confirmed microscopically. Sarcoptic.	J.O.T.

Army Form C. 2118.

WAR DIARY
or
INTELLIGENCE SUMMARY.
(Erase heading not required.)

A.D.V.S.
16th Divⁿ

Instructions regarding War Diaries and Intelligence Summaries are contained in F.S. Regs., Part II. and the Staff Manual respectively. Title pages will be prepared in manuscript.

Place	Date	Hour	Summary of Events and Information	Remarks and references to Appendices
LILLERS	15.3.16	10 am	Visited 182nd, 180th, 177th, 173rd O.R. Ser at BELLERY, AMES, LIERES & ECCEDECQUES. As a rule there are no arrangements for clipping. A.D.O.S. arranging to send up 4 clipping machines.	J.O.A
	16.3.16	10 am	Visited M.P. 4/143 EOY Train - RAIMBERT.	
		10.30 am	Inspected 6th Regl. Drink Pgh - BURBURG - condition very good	
		11 am	6th Cavalry W. Repn - ALLOUAGNE - condⁿ very good, arrangements to	
		11.30 am	Visited 9th Bde. two - LAPUGNOY. & inspected 3 remounts sent to 43rd Inf. Pgr - are 14 h. mules, supposed to be night forwards fit for work, but condition not good - all tucky.	J.O.A
		2 pm	Visited Agr. Remount Section - BONNEHEM.	
		4 pm	The 1 Sectn. 4. Rgo. Park - BAS RIEUX.	
	17.3.16	10 am	47 Tn. V.S. & report. 13 Amm. Col. at B.R.I. Army at R.M. HQ gre ECCEDECQUES,	
		12 noon	Inspected H.2 Section, 4. Reserve Park at BAS RIEUX - condⁿ casting annuals of for Remount releases.	
		2.30 pm	Conference of V.Os. Chocqueury Rd.	
	18.3.16	10.30 am	Inspected 156 Field COY. R.E. - LAPUGNOY - condition horses good - chilorown - shoeing Sat, feet to toe. Condⁿ hunfers Two - Condⁿ hnfantry good	J.O.A
		11 am	Inspect of Mr Dublin Fus - Couchy - home, shoeing poor	

WAR DIARY or INTELLIGENCE SUMMARY

Army Form C. 2118.

(6)

A.D.M.S.
16th Division

Place	Date	Hour	Summary of Events and Information	Remarks and references to Appendices
LIUERS.	18/3/16	3 pm	Inspected 112 L Fld Ambulance - good condition, but dirty & loury. Showery.	J.O.H.
	19/3/16	12.45pm	4) M.S. evacuated 22 wounded, retaining 2/122 E.R.S.	
	20/3/16		4) M.S. evacuated 16 wounded and 2/112 E.R.S. Statistics for the Division.	
			Two sick - temperature - admitted to M.V.S.	
			4) Fd M.S. received three Reinforcements - two riding 1 L.D. Shipments are sent to unit today.	J.O.H.
	21/3/16	10.30am	Inspected 143 & 144 Co's A.D.C.	
		11 am	Visited the Gros, 49th Inf. Bde. - RAIMBERT. Drugs from the Base are being committed by delays. 0/c A.D.V. Stores states that the consignments have been preferred through A.M.F.O. Mbren	J.O.H.
			attached H.P. animals, M.M.P. & Sig. Co's Rec. Coal	
			4) M.S. evacuated 8 wounded.	
	22/3/16	9 am	To NORRENT-FONTES & BERGUETTE - inspection of two Horse Cpl Behie by 25th Div. A.D.S. 15th Div. called arrangements on the Division changing over.	
		11 am		
			From Camiat Peong the maps from 48th Inf. Bde. employed indiscriminately	J.O.H.

Army Form C. 2118.

WAR DIARY
or
INTELLIGENCE SUMMARY.
(Erase heading not required.)

A.D.V.S.
16th Divn.

Place	Date	Hour	Summary of Events and Information	Remarks and references to Appendices
LILLERS.	23.2.16	10 am	Inspect 7th Sinks two. - RAIMBERT conditions bad, though fair	
		11.15	" 8th " " - " good	
		12 nn	" 7th " " - CAUCHY-a-LA-TOUR " fair	
		3 pm	Visited D.A.C. - LECTURES.	
	24.3.16	11 am	Inspect 137 Field AMB. R.E. - REVEILLON - conditions good -	fair staff
		2.30pm	Conference of V.O.s	
	25.3.16	11 am	To REBECQ to collect 3 horses left by 33rd D.A.C. Detachment of 47 Div. V.S. had brought in previous evening.	
		pm	Visited 180th, 150th & 177th Bdes R.F.A. 25 horses evacuated by 47 Div. V.S.	JRH
	26.3.16	9 am	To BETHUNE with F.D.A.D.V.S. and purchase of horses for two artillery brigades.	
		pm	Visit these two units. 7 horses evacuated by 47 Div.	
		4.15 pm	Sgt SAYER reports for duty with H.Q. 47 Divn. R.S. relief of Capt WILSHAW D.A.V.S.	JRH
	27.3.16	10 am	Leave by car with H.Q. the Division, stop at BETHUNE, finish D.A.D.V.S. the Division purchase horses for two brigades R.F.A.	JRH

Army Form C. 2118.

WAR DIARY
or
INTELLIGENCE SUMMARY.

(Erase heading not required.)

A.D.V.S.
16th Division

Place	Date	Hour	Summary of Events and Information	Remarks and references to Appendices
NOEUX-LES-MINES.	27/3/16	12 noon	Arrive with H.Q. the Division, in charge of 16th Division, 47 m.v.s. arrives, taking over 2 sick animals left behind by 18th Div? M.v.s.	
		2 pm	Visits lines of 47th, 48th & 49th Inf. Bdes.	f.o.A.
	28/3/16.	am.	Saw mules - doubtful mules to Stadium (3rd time tested) 72nd B.R.T.A	
		pm	attached to this Division. Control by Subventionaire that at 12th horse. - at VERQUIN	
			Visit 3rd Heavy Bde. - HOUCHIN	f.o.A
	29/3/16	9:30am	Destroy mule - VERQUIN. - Pts showing of Condors and when not build - but no success in air pulmonary apparently of recent infection. Visit Brit Trench at VAUDRICOURT	
			Visit 157 Coy R.A & 11th Hants. - MAZINGARBE	f.o.A
	30/3/16	9:30am	Inspect horses of 71st 72nd 73rd B.R.T.A - attached 16 th Div	f.o.A
			All Aug got after two months in the line.	
		4pm	Visit 46th B & Bn. 9, Coy - BOSNAY & H.Q. 4th Reserve Park - HESDIGNEUL	
	31/3/16	am	Inspect 157, 178, 18 th Field Coys R.E. - MAZINGARBE.	f.o.A
		pm	Conference at V.O.S obtaining arrangement for animals of the new Div. Reinvey has Report submitted to D.A.Q.m.g.	
			47 m.v.S. evacuate 7 animals.	

J. Andrews
Major a.v.c

Army Form C. 2118.

WAR DIARY
or
INTELLIGENCE SUMMARY.
(Erase heading not required.)

A.D.V.S. 16th Divn

Vol 5

Place	Date	Hour	Summary of Events and Information	Remarks and references to Appendices
NOEUX-LES-MINES	1.4.16	am	Inspect 70th Bde R.F.A. & 6th Heavy Bde at NOEUX.	
		4pm	"C" Batty 7th Bde attacked for cond. bad & work. 111th & 112th Heavy Batteries - HOUCHIN.	
	2.4.16	am	Make arrangements re supply of tobacco & watering troughs of Inf. Bde.	
	3.4.16	am	Inspect 1st Machine Gun Squadron & 1st Sect. 4th Res. Pk. tr. - GOSNAY. Review of horses, harness & saddles. Grazing by enemy. & to large pinhead.	
			16th D.V. All Artillery annual rtn. this area by return. Visit 15th D.A.C.I. HESDIGNEUL	
	4.4.16	am	47th V.S. arcenal ?21 animals. Inspect annuals of 111th, 112th & 113th Fd Ambulances. Cardgen co?. stpt 110 & F.A. cloning up stpt 112 & A. Visit horse lines of all infantry Battalions. Improvement	
		pm	Henry Cavl. Alls annual now being carried ? visiting of Batts.	
		3am	Capt. HOWE & horse took 4 hrs walk by shell fire which ? record horse badly wounded when ? brown before dawn.	
	6.4.16 to 14.4.16		On leave in England. Delayed at FOLKESTONE + BOULOGNE on return journey 47th V.S. animal rtn.20 annuals.6th - 8th October 1st - 721 on the 12th week	
	14.4.16	10pm	arrive NOEUX-LES-MINES.	

WAR DIARY
or
INTELLIGENCE SUMMARY

Army Form C. 2118.

A.D.V.S. 16th Division

Place	Date	Hour	Summary of Events and Information	Remarks and references to Appendices
NOEUX LES MINES	15.4.16		15th Divl Artillery are moving into this area.	
		pm	Motored out and proceeded to VERQUIN, where some of 2nd D.A.C. had pitched, owing to arrival earlier of 9 Cavalry having occurred without escort.	
		5pm	To BEUVRY. To see Capt. THOMPSON A.V.C. in charge of Heavy Artillery Horses, & his officers & a men & H.Q. 9 H.A.G.	J.A.T.
	16.4.16	am	Visited Billets of 16th D.A. where horses arrived this am.	
		3pm	A'noon conference at A.D.V.S. at 1st Army H.Q.	J.A.T.
	17.4.16	am	Visited the Batteries of 16th D.A. Capt REID, & Lieut. LUCKING & McMAHON, report their arrival & billets are not satisfactory. The men of Artillery in most cases billetted.	J.A.T.
	18.4.16	9.30am	Inspected 177th Bde. R.F.A.	
		2.30pm	182nd Bde. R.F.A.	
		4pm	No. N.S. wagons & animals. O.C. Sanitary Section has arranged to inspect horses & all billets vacated by the Artillery which have moved out, & they are busy up to date.	J.A.T.
	19.4.16	am	Inspected 150th & 177th Bdes. R.F.A.	
		noon	B.V.S. 1st Army called.	
		4pm	Inspected two wagon teams in 2nd Siege Battery, reported him to have one lame	
			47th N.V.S. wagons to 4.D. animals arrived.	J.A.T.

The D.A.G.   SECRET
3rd Echelon

Herewith "War Diary" for
the month of May 1916

           Jo Andrews
             Major. A.V.C.
        A.D.V.S. 16th Division

3/6/16

WAR DIARY
or
INTELLIGENCE SUMMARY.
(Erase heading not required.)

Army Form C. 2118.

A.D.V.S. 16th Division

Place	Date	Hour	Summary of Events and Information	Remarks and references to Appendices
NOEUX-LES-MINES	1.5.16	am	Inspected 2nd Siege Battery, 147th & 148th M.G. Corps, horses 1st & 2nd (S). Fie & Corps R.E. - MAZINGARBE.	
		pm	Inspected 49th M.G. Corps, horses 117 & 138. Hay ration — horses in showing & condition of animals of M.C. Corps arrived from England very poor. A showing contingent arrived too late to be photoed before arrival and leaving of M.C. Corps. Stamina all turned of 146th R.A.M.C. R.G.A. for the horses — 2 suspected mange cases, which fail inspection mainly on examination of parts chafed at ears of harness.	J.A.
	2.5.16	11.30 am	Inspected 142 Bty. A.V.C.	J.A.
		pm	47 M.V.S. evacuate 8 animals.	
	3.5.16	noon	Inspected 77 & 160th Bdes. R.F.A. — Stable management of A.V.O. very G.A.D.	
		2.30 pm	Attend lecture by transport.	
		6 pm	Visit H.Q. 4th Res. Park re veterinary equipment. 47 M.V.S. evacuate 8 animals & that BROAD A.V.C. & Jow Lau.	J.A.
	4.5.16	am	Inspected 177th R. Bdy. & part of 182 Bdy. R.F.A.	
		pm	47 M.V.S. evacuate 8 animals. Co	J.A.
	5.5.16	am	Visit veterinary camp with Staff Captain R.A. 47 M.V.S. evacuate 24 animals.	J.A.

Army Form C. 2118.

WAR DIARY
INTELLIGENCE SUMMARY
(Erase heading not required.)

A.D.V.S.
16th Div.

(3.)

Place	Date	Hour	Summary of Events and Information	Remarks and references to Appendices
NOEUX- LES- MINES	13/5/16	a.m.	At 4) hrs. 2 cows turned out R.A. wagon lines.	
		2 p.m.	Section 36 annuals for Farm.	
		4.30 p.m.	Visit Office of A.D.V.S. 16th Div.	
	14.5.16	a.m.	Visit H.Q. R.A. & 1st Corps R.G.A., also 180 & 177 & 177 & 29 Div	
			at MAZINGARBE & LES BREBIS	OA
		p.m.	Inspect all Infantry Transport	
	15.5.16		A Coy of Engineers, inspected from A. Batty. 10ppt Rest. LENTON Ave. in two farms, 9 days in one to	OA
		a.m.	all horses at 180 Bde. melting. Inspect 177 & 180 B.A.Cos, vans & ability careful to Inspect A.B.&D. Batteries 182 Bde R.F.A	OA
		p.m.	visited office of A.D.V.S. 16th Div.	
	16/5/16	9 a.m.	Inspect A. 180 Bde. melting carried on A.B.&C. Bats yc. 177 4 Bde. vans & ability carried on	OA
		10 a.m.	visit F.E.I. Adv. Remount Section	
	17/5/16	10 a.m.	Inspect A. Battery 180th Bde. reparture in Surface of 177 Bde. going to all Camp rick	OA
		10.30am	Watch D.A.P.mg & C.R.E. round artillery times in Bryan	
		11.30 a.m.	cases of suitable transport 180th R.a. 6 & A. Batty.	
		3 p.m.	See cases of "tetable" horses 180 R.A. 6 & A. Batty Icaning to tulip" Poisoning, lands cil. Symptoms very slight	

Army Form C. 2118.

WAR DIARY
or
INTELLIGENCE SUMMARY.
(Erase heading not required.)

A.D.M.S.
16th Divn.

(A)

Instructions regarding War Diaries and Intelligence Summaries are contained in F. S. Regs., Part II and the Staff Manual respectively. Title pages will be prepared in manuscript.

Place	Date	Hour	Summary of Events and Information	Remarks and references to Appendices
NOEUX -LES- MINES	18.5.16	am	Visit artillery waggon lines	JoA
		pm	Take samples of water from 180th Bde. R.F.A. H.Q. & army for analysis.	
	19.5.16	7.30am	P.M. on two poisoning cases at 180th Bde. - gastritis.	JoA
		9am	Neputitis. Chief from signal Coy.	
			Old D.R. under artillery wire.	
		2.30pm	Conference at V.O.P.	
		4.30pm	to H.Q. 16th D.A.C. to see O.C. re reorganization of B.A.C. & D.A.C.	JoA
	20.4.16	am	Inspect 112 Fd. Ambulance, 4 M.G. Coy. & Labour Coy.	
		3pm	Visit troops at VERQUIN.	JoA
			47 tents wanted to 22 annexes.	
	21.5.16	9pm	Inspect 1 R.I.A.D. & 1 H.D. from each Fd. Ambulance	
			transfer to each M.G. Coys: the H.D. being ready	JoA
			by Rehearse to for L.D.s	
		5pm	Lawn shield spring.	
	22.5.16	am	Inspect men sent at 148th Bty. R.g.a. Vermelles thence	JoA
			inspect E.D. Exchanges S.2.H. - & houses from	

Army Form C. 2118.

WAR DIARY
or
INTELLIGENCE SUMMARY.
(Erase heading not required.)

A.D.V.S.
16 H Div.

Instructions regarding War Diaries and Intelligence Summaries are contained in F.S. Regs., Part II. and the Staff Manual respectively. Title pages will be prepared in manuscript.

Place	Date	Hour	Summary of Events and Information	Remarks and references to Appendices
NOEUX- LES- MINES.	23.3.16	9am	Inspect selected grouping horses, visited O.C. 16 D.A.C., conformation of R.A. & D.A.C. Inspect 48 & 49 By MG Coys.	LotA
	24.3.16	9am	all surplus R.A. transport horses for inspection & classified by D.A.Q.M.G. my staff	LotA
			47 nurs were to 4A animals	
	25.3.16	am	Inspect 3rd Corps R.I. & 11th Ham tps - Mazingarbe	
			12t Battery R.G.A. & unit 111 R.Balty Reg.a	
			Visit H.Q. horse lines 180 – B.R. – afternoon	
		5pm	town & hilled killed. about 20 wounded by the affair	
	26.3.16	am	Inspect A Batty. 180 HRS - in mules going - my visit	
			Visit R.A. wagon lines	
		3pm	Conference of V.O.s	
			Visit Army of D. Stations 77 A & 182 → B3rd VERQUIN	
		4.30p	A.Mt Fleury C.A.S.E. arm'd to take up new effects	
			from Capt. Kerr Avc.	
			Capt. Reid A.V.C - have come in ex	
			V.Luth A Barty No 4 B.R. & him to E. Swadlen. S.D.H.M.	
	27.3.16 am		can't leave	LotA

Army Form C. 2118.

WAR DIARY
or
INTELLIGENCE SUMMARY.
(Erase heading not required.)

A.D.V.S.
16th DNS

Place	Date	Hour	Summary of Events and Information	Remarks and references to Appendices
NOEUX-LES-MINES.	28/5/16	am	Visit to R.A. map Bureau.	OH
	29/5/16	am	Visit 'B' Echelon DAC - HESDIGNEUL, & transport H.Q. sub & the Park - GOSNAY.	OH
	30/5/16	noon	Visit H.Q. transport two & 150th Bde. R.F.A. - MAZINGARBE. Selected injured 2.2.20 48 - Aux 36B. No ambulance for advanced collecting post for No. 1 St. attempt	lost
	2 pm		met A.D.D.R. 1st Army to 142 Cav. A.D.C. train ambulance preparing for entering.	
	5.30 pm		Conference of VOs in alteration of disposal of units to ensure one for handing of DACS.	
			A D.V.S. 1st Army called, in view of picked up males in divns. Both collecting units are placed at disposal of Demp. for H.Q. & all trails are drawn from the horse troop & from same for transport of D.V.S. supplies to 47 Divs.	
	3 pm		Inspected 49th Inf. Bde - Shortage of Birkshire Reg't (carts & two mules) & 1st Lincolns (two). Moving bad. 47 D.V.S. moved 510 animals.	
	31/5/16	11 am	POISONING - 100 horses affected & 4 died unsightly due to control fan. Change analysed but was delegation. A full report has been sent to ADD.VS. 1st Army. Evacuations - an average amount to the forth this period 310 animals. This appears very satisfactory compared with past forth. Samples on management of R.D.C.S. + D.A.C. are recommended from the Sqn by Mr. A. Anderson	

1b-253. Wt. W2541/1454 200,000 5/15 D.D.&L. (APSS/Forms/C.2118.

The
D.A.G.
3rd Echelon

Herewith 'War Diary' for
month of June 1916

J. Andrews
Major A.V.C.
A.D.V.S. 16th Division

1.7.16

Army Form C. 2118.

WAR DIARY
or
INTELLIGENCE SUMMARY.
(Erase heading not required.)

A.D.V.S.
16th Division
Vol 7

Instructions regarding War Diaries and Intelligence Summaries are contained in F.S. Regs., Part II. and the Staff Manual respectively. Title pages will be prepared in manuscript.

Place	Date	Hour	Summary of Events and Information	Remarks and references to Appendices
NOEUX-LES-MINES	1.6.16	am	Visit R.A. wagon lines. Inspect all Veterinary equipment, sent for instruments etc. to complete units. Inspect 47 & 48 Inf. Bde. Condition of animals at Divn. transport is very good, shoeing good, weights of teams the Regt. & Small Arms Amm. transport are bad, chiefly of animals of previous trek to trenches.	App. I
		pm	Inspect 111 E. 134 & 140 Batteries R.G.A. shewing rural ends of their animals have recently improved. Capt. HUTTON states he will inspect a platoon wk.	App. I
	2.6.16	am		
		3pm	Conference of 4.00 Captn. READ A.V.C. returning from leave.	App. I
	3.6.16	am	Visit R.A. wagon lines at NOEUX-LES-MINES + VERQUIN. Inspect 49 H.M.G. Coy. All their M.G. Coys have recently improved. All working conditions above & at works of their animals remain very poor. Conditions & their shewing many good subjects.	App. I
	4.6.16	am	Inspect 47 H.M.G. Coy	
		3pm	Attend conference of ADs V.S. at 1st ARMY Hd. Qrs. Lieut. McMAHON A.V.C. admitted to No. 112 F.A. & wounded to No. 33. C.C.S. continues on to training ricks. Probable duration of return 10-14 days.	App. I
	5.6.16	am	Visit by Bd. TRA. wagon lines. Call for lists of equip. shewing from R.A.F.	App. I
	6.6.16	am	Inspect all counts at MAZINGARBE. Capt. READ A.V.C. was visited wks in charge of the former area. R.F.A. no more till this return.	App. I
		pm	47 M.V.S. evacuate 13 cases.	
	7.6.16	am	Horse 7.C. 32.-138 Batty R.G.A. marked to medicine glanders confirmed by post-mortem. Have informed concerns in his armies here. A malleined column carrying orders but was to arrive over from D.V.S., 1st ARMY.	App. I
		3pm		

Army Form C. 2118.

WAR DIARY
or
INTELLIGENCE SUMMARY.
(Erase heading not required.)

A.D.V.S
16th Div[ision]

(2)

Place	Date	Hour	Summary of Events and Information	Remarks and references to Appendices
NOEUX-LES-MINES	8.6.16	am	Inspect No. 1. Section. 4th Res. Pk. — GOSNAY:- Examine a horse cast & choking, with violent attempts at rumination. Sick 12 horses, — 2 prs. Auscultation fair relief in the horses. Visit transport of 11th Trench Mortar & 8th Rgt. Two from 12th Brit. Brown infoplants new salomony materially remaining. Sample for ruk and LABOURSE troops. Lubricate OARSF mg. 9.	J.S.A.
	9.6.16	pm	Conference of V.O.P.	J.S.A.
		2.30pm	47 An. V.S. watercart & camp.	J.S.A.
	10.6.16	am	Inspect A 177. M 80. — Ruthyp. visit R-A waggon horse	
		pm	Lieut McMahon A.V.C. intro to Sub by from the 1. C.C.S.	J.S.A.
	11.6.16	am	Inspect A 77. & 170 Trench Mg. Bty.	J.S.A.
		pm	Report on number of sound, capped / cracked salmon removals Vets Walkito D.D.V.S	J.S.A.
	12.6.16	9 am	Em. BETHUNE with D.D.V.S. to visit veterinary hospitals &	J.S.A.
			ABBEVILLE.	
	13.6.16	1 pm	Return. 47 M.V.S. evans to 10 camps.	
		aft	Visit DADOS. purchases of crushers for artillery trip Brown.	
		2 pm	Interview C.R.A. re pickets up mud cartery	
		3 pm	With staff Capt. R.A. to select surplus horses from 77 & 178.	
			Brown & same to 182 & 180.	
		5.30pm	Inspect & refile walkets & picketing of 4th Echn & blue Sup Road	J.S.A.
			& 77 & 4th Bde. R.F.A.	
	14.6.16	am	Inspect 162 & R & R & R. ten — great improvement.	
		pm	Inspect 153 & 152. & Corp — MAZANGARBE — stable management	J.S.A.

Army Form C. 2118.

WAR DIARY
or
INTELLIGENCE SUMMARY.
(Erase heading not required.)

A.D.V.S.
16th Divn.

Instructions regarding War Diaries and Intelligence Summaries are contained in F.S. Regs., Part II. and the Staff Manual respectively. Title pages will be prepared in manuscript.

Place	Date	Hour	Summary of Events and Information	Remarks and references to Appendices
NOEUX-LES-MINES	15.6.16.	a.m.	Inspect 5.100th Fd.Bde. - Lines still poor in "A" Battery. Visit Inf. Transport Lines.	J.O.A.
		p.m.	47 m.V.S. inspected. 13 cases.	
	16.6.16	11.30 am	D.D.V.S. 1st army, inspects m.V.S.	
		2.30 pm	Conference at VOS.	
	17.6.16	a.m.	Inspect 177 Fd.Amb. R.F.A.	J.O.A.
		p.m.	Visit Mounted Inf. Transport Lines.	
	18.6.16	a.m.	With O.C. 47 m.V.S. to MAZINGARBE, interview Town Major & Mayor re site for Advanced Collecting Station for m.V.S.- Existing station at cross roads (Map 36B. L29.a.5.9) Interviewed A.D.V.S. 15th Division at LABOURSE.	J.O.A.
	19.6.16	p.m.	Inspect 77 Fd.Bde. R.F.A. Visit Inf. Transport Lines.	J.O.A.
	20.6.16	a.m.	47 m.V.S. Inspected, 12 cases. Inspect A Echelon 16th D.A.C. at VERQUIN - good.	J.O.A.
		2pm	Inspect 119 Reserve Pk. receiving for the Division.	
	21.6.16	a.m.	Inspect "B" Echelon D.A.C. & H.Q. & H.A.I. Section of 4th Reserve Park.	J.O.A.
		3 pm	Corps Commander inspects R.A. wagon lines.	
	22.6.16	a.m.	Visit 143, 144, 145 Coys. But Train, & surface lines; very flat horses in lines. A number of horses from 40th Divn. Taken attacks are in poor condition; & esp. Mangey.	J.O.A.
		pm	Inspect 48th Inf. Bde., Transport lines & convoys; cannot by day. In my opinion one 2nd rate Artillery attack of m.M.V.S. inspected 13 cases.	
		6 pm	Serious Epidemic of Thrush. D.D. & D.L. of S.S. M. of E.C.F.S.D. - Rupture colon, due to large amount of windsucke's Clay. 47 m.V.S. inspected 13 cases.	J.O.A.

Army Form C. 2118.

WAR DIARY
or
INTELLIGENCE SUMMARY
(Erase heading not required.)

A.D.V.S. 16th Div.

(5)

Instructions regarding War Diaries and Intelligence Summaries are contained in F.S. Regs., Part II. and the Staff Manual respectively. Title pages will be prepared in manuscript.

Place	Date	Hour	Summary of Events and Information	Remarks and references to Appendices
NOEUX-LES-MINES.	30.6.16	a.m.	Conference of V.D.O. Mobilizing of 40th Divl. Artillery commenced. Inspect in of Fd. Ambulance - improvement reported throughout. All veterinary equipment (Water troughs & buckets) of the Division has been thoroughly overhauled during the wks & all deficiencies replaced, & chr. to fields. There is little doubt that Fd. Kitchens are still the most important source of undue wear & tear on the roads. Stopping and hooking on and off for being turned, before the mules can util being packed, loading and moving practically all made hard on the roads are bound & packing rails.	J.A.

J. Andrews
Major
A.D.V.L 16th Div.

WAR DIARY or **INTELLIGENCE SUMMARY**

Army Form C. 2118.

A.D.V.S.
16th Division

Place	Date	Hour	Summary of Events and Information	Remarks and references to Appendices
NOEUX-LES-MINES	1.7.16	a.m.	To Ordnance workshop - LABEUVRIÈRE, in repair of M.V.S. limbered wagon.	J.H.
		p.m.	Visit 111th & 135th Bakeries R.G.A.	
	2.7.16	a.m.	47. Tn. V.S. inspect 11 animals. Inspect sick animals casts - 48th & 2nd Inf. Bde. animals & 49th Inf. Bde. Conference of A.Ds.V.S. at AIRE	J.H.
	3.7.16	a.m.	Inspect "A" Battery, 7th Bde. Visit returning of 40th D.A. which marches to area today.	J.H.
			Arranged Fd.H.Q. for 153 & 156. Cav Res & 11th Hants. Remove to new horse lines from MAZINGARBE, the two taken by shell-fire in two days, several wounded.	
			To LABOURSE - called at office of A.D.V.S. 15th Divn.	
	4.7.16	p.m.	Round artillery wagon-lines with C.R.E. in the way of finding shelters for lathing sick lines.	J.H.
			47. Tn. V.S. checks 72 animals.	
	5.7.16	a.m.	Visit 1st Corps Cavalry at VAUDRICOURT, inspect & see turning arrangements. Report to entrance to S.Div.S. 1st Army.	J.H.
			Inspect 63 Remount animals for the Division.	
	6.7.16	a.m.	Visit R.A. wagon lines, make arrangements to	J.H.
		pm.	47.Tn.V.S. invects 9 animals. Lieut. McMAHON reports for duty.	J.H.
	7.7.16	a.m.	Visit R.A. wagon lines & see C.O. of Bn. C Sqn. C Coy.	J.H.
			Conference at V.O.S. Capt Rhind. A.V.C. France from MAZINGARBE.	J.H.

NOEUX-LES-MINES.

Army Form C. 2118.

WAR DIARY
~~INTELLIGENCE SUMMARY~~
(Erase heading not required.)

A.D.V.S.
16th Division

Instructions regarding War Diaries and Intelligence Summaries are contained in F.S. Regs., Part II. and the Staff Manual respectively. Title pages will be prepared in manuscript.

Place	Date	Hour	Summary of Events and Information	Remarks and references to Appendices
NOEUX-LES-MINES.	8.7.16	a.m.	Inspect F. 47 Inf. Bde. Interview A.D.V.S. 40th Division	for A.
		pm	Inspect D. 17 & C. 77 - VERQUIN.	
	9.7.16	a.m.	Inspect & re-classify horses of 113th Field Ambulance, an extensive outbreak of mange in this unit, handle microscopical examination of the rashes & skin scrapings. Infection. Send two cases to M.V.S. 7	
			Inspect 47th M.G. Coy. - improvement.	
		pm	Inspect animals of 16th Div. Train. - Condition excellent, shoeing in fair cases requires improvement.	
			Lieut. F. BROAD A.V.C. instructed to carry out to-day visit & change of 1st Corps cycling Batt. - 6 horses at 16 horses.	for A.
	10.7.16	am	Inspect 71st, 91st Stat. & 4th Reserve Park, & 1st Army Auxiliary Horse Transport Company. Horses of former there out condition	
			weak, fly. Visit Regtl. Officers BETHUNE, re evacuations in Infirmaries.	for A.
		5 pm	4) M.V.S.	
		1.30 pm	M.V.S. made a tour to train sick at NOEUX station, owing to be staff.	for A.
	11.7.16	am	Inspect (87-975) Corps. R.E. - MAZINGARBE. Inspected loads of mess chateau MAZINGARBE to Rue d'ARRAS, no forcible work & fair evacuation of sick from agreed collecting stations.	
		pm	47 M.V.S. evacuated 23 animals Co.	for A.
	12.7.16	am	Inspect 47) 4 Bde. M.G. Coy & 13 Batty 77 4th Bde. Visit A.T.7 Bde. & 113 4th F.A.	for off.
	13.7.16	am	Infectious camps Circus B.177, B.180, D.180, D.182, & D.77. - Great improvement.	
		pm	4) M.V.S. evacuated 12 animals.	for A.
	14.7.16	am	Inspect 112 F.A.	
		3 pm	Conference of V.O's	
		5 pm	Visit 2534 X 274 NF 200 D.D. & L. A.D.S.S IV Corps 211 BONNEHEM. - inspect horses sent to	for A.
			Composite 113 F.A.	

Army Form C. 2118.

WAR DIARY
or
INTELLIGENCE SUMMARY.
(Erase heading not required.)

A.D.V.S.
16th Division

Place	Date	Hour	Summary of Events and Information	Remarks and references to Appendices
NOEUX-LES-MINES	15/7/16	am	Visit Divl. Train, veterinary cases aeg. & sub. to D.A.C. 47 H.M.G. Coy. went to cinema. Lieut. Col. BETHUNE 47 MVS evacuated 11 animals. D.77 move to BEUVRY. — A.D.V.S. & Brn. inspected Remounts to at 113 th F.A. Saw two suspected vicious animals from this horses at 48 M.G. Coy. Report on cases to D.H.Q.	J.H.
	16/7/16	am	Visit 48th Inf. Bde. Transport lines. Saw & inspected 47th War Biary for truing to D.A.C. the Brn. Report on proper distribution of Mountain & 7 lines & tn. to D.D.R. & Aly. found BROAD inspected condition of horses of No 1 Sect'n 48 Res. Pk.	
	17/7/16	am	Inspect 70 & 1 Sect'n 47th Res. Pk., interview C.O. also up from O.C. Train of poor condition of horses.	J.H.
	18/7/16	am	Inspect A/180 Bde., still several thin horses remaining. Visit C/180 Bde & 156 Cay. R.E.	
		pm	Inspect No 1 Sect 4 47th Res. Pk. with O.C. train, who arranges to give their horses a week in rest. Visit No 2 Sect 4 Remm 1 Sect'n. — GONNEHEM, in ckarge of own transp. of own transport horses. 47 Mk.V.S. evacu t 22 animals.	J.H.
	19/7/16	am	Attend a meeting of Divisional Commander at R.A. on Aline. — Also trench mortars AT C.177 AT B.180.	
		pm	Attended station 9.20 to 10.30 to inspect remounts to arriving for the Division.	J.H.

WAR DIARY / INTELLIGENCE SUMMARY

Army Form C. 2118.

A.D.V.S. 16th Div.

Place	Date	Hour	Summary of Events and Information	Remarks and references to Appendices
NOEUX-LES-MINES	20/7/16	10.30am	Inspect 140th Bakery R.G.A; + Pick & up 'Debility' cases for evacuation	JoH
		11.30am	Inspect 117th Bakery R.G.A	JoH
		12 noon	Inspect 1 & 2 Sec Fd.16th D.A.C. Construct funnels, evacuate	JoH
			Inspect 1st, 2nd & 3rd 1st Cav. Fd. Amb. MAZINGARBE. Also H.Q. 18th & 13th Bde.	
	21/7/16	am	Interview A.D.V.S 40th Div	JoH
		3pm	Conference of V.Os	JoH
	22/7/16	am	Inspect A.T.13, F.62. Bde, A.177 & D.182. Sent afresh detailed terms for evacuation	
			15th Div. H.Q. move to front left area	
		pm	Interview A.D.V.S. France Div.	JoH
			4) Mt.V.S. vacant. 12 animals.	
	23/7/16	10am	Report to G.O.C. unfit work in town.	
			Inspect (4) 2nd Inf Bde. + M.G. Coy	JoH
		2.30pm	Examine 35 mules H.D. 16th Bn L Pioneers	
		2.30pm	Examine 35 mules at CONNEHEM. + Horses for transfer to CONNEHEM.	
			Inspect C.117. Bde. eva.d Debility cases for evacuation to transfer	JoH
	24/7/16	am	Inspect 48 H. M.G.Coy. 111 + 113 + Fd Amb.	
			Transfer & recharge of 48 Inf Bde 133 from Capt Howe to Capt Reid A.V.C.	JoH
		pm	4) Mt V.S. evacuate 21 animals.	

WAR DIARY or INTELLIGENCE SUMMARY

Army Form C. 2118.

A.D.V.S.
16th Divn.

Place	Date	Hour	Summary of Events and Information	Remarks and references to Appendices
NOEUX-LES-MINES	25/7/16	a.m.	Inspected A, B & C 150 Bde, and "Mobility" cares for mules to Inspected A, B, C & D 182 Bde — mules were made unsteady to LABOURET & VERQUINEUL — Conditions throughout satisfy. Interview A.D.V.S. 8th Divn.	J.H.
	26/7/16	a.m.	Served orders of inspection to arrange with Bn. Vet. Inspected N.T. Section 4th Res. Pk. with L.O.C. Some great improvement. Orders to fix animals in another unit.	
		p.m.	Visit 11th Hants 47th Inf Bde & 49th M.G. Coy Lucous. O.O.C. orders new cooking arrangements to be made at N.T.S.	J.H.
	27/7/16	a.m.	47th M.V.S. evacuate Fr. V.23 animals. Inspected 114th Hants Bn, 49th Inf Bde, & D)) Bde.	
		p.m.	Inspected 143 Coy A.S.C.	J.H.
	28/7/16	p.m.	47 M.V.S. evacuate Fr. 14 animals. Some lame & wounded by shellfire.	J.H.
	29/7/16	a.m.	Inspected 156 Coy R.F. & B)) Bde. 4/56 Coy R.F. Visit a)) Bde.	J.H.
	30/7/16	a.m.	Inspected 112th F.A. D)) Bde & C)) Bde.	J.H.
		p.m.	Reply to G.O.C. 48th Inf Bde in letter supervision of his Ride	J.H.
			47 M.V.S. evacuate 8 animals	

WAR DIARY.

A.D.V.S. 16th Division

MONTH OF AUGUST, 1916.

VOLUME:- 9.

WAR DIARY / INTELLIGENCE SUMMARY

Army Form C. 2118.

A.D.V.S.
16th Divn.

Place	Date	Hour	Summary of Events and Information	Remarks and references to Appendices
NOEUX-LES-MINES	6.8.16	am	Inspect 47th & 49th Inf. Bdrs.	JOA
		pm	Attend conference of A.D.V.S. at Army H.Q.	
	7.8.16	am	Inspect attchmnt. to 6th MAZINGARBE, 47 & 13182 Bdr. 10 horses of Div'l Train killed in BETHUNE by shell fire.	JOA
		pm	Visit 49th Inf. Bdr. Transport lines.	
	8.8.16	am	47 Tn. V.S. evacuate 8 animals. Inspect No. 4 Section 16th D.A.C.	JOA
		pm	Inspect 142 Cav. A.V.C.	
	9.8.16		With A.D.V.S. I 8th & 32nd Divns, visit Base V.P. & Hospitals (3) at ABBEVILLE. Interview with D.V.S.	JOA
	10.8.16	am	Inspect B.17 Bdr. R.F.A., A.B. & C.180 Bdr. A.13 & D.77 & R.F.A. Visit 143 Cav. A.V.C. the 4 cases of suppos'd glanders, two eventually determined symptomsonly marked within cords.	JOA
	11.8.16	9.30am	Mad R.M. examined two at Div'l. Train and one at 47 Tn. Horse examined cases. Acute Laryngitis & conjunctival catarrh appears only symptoms. Careful examination of infra-parotids, no adenocephalo l. lymph glands. Operation taken two to officers on legs. Conference of D.V.S. & 4 Twn. V.S. + Evens at 8 animals.	JOA

Army Form C. 2118.

WAR DIARY
or
INTELLIGENCE SUMMARY.
(Erase heading not required.)

A.D.v.S
16th Div.

Place	Date	Hour	Summary of Events and Information	Remarks and references to Appendices
NOEUX-LES-MINES	12.8.16	a.m.	Inspect 11th Hants, 17th Northumberland Fus (from 32nd Div?) & 96th M.G. Coy (32nd Div.) showing two establishments very bad. Visit 48th Inf. Bde – a case of scarlet. Inspect new 48th M.G. Coy.	O.H
	13.8.16	"	Interview with A.D.v.S. 8th Div.	O.H
		a.m.	Inspect C(17) Bde, 48th Inf Bde & M.G. Coy 111 & 113 of 2nd Amb. Visit Div. & train four two men running forward carrying one man, which one recovering slowly.	O.H
	14.8.16	a.m.	Inspect H.Q. & No. 1 Sect. 4 of Res. Park. 2 taenia, skin scaly with microscope. Several cases of scabies, infants have occurred recently in different units.	O.H
	15.8.16	a.m.	Inspect F.A. & P. 180 Bde & 156 Coy. R.E. Interview O.C. 182 Bde. Examine all horses of C(17) Bde & C182 Bde for chain sweat – unfavourable result.	O.H
		p.m.	4) N.v.S. evacuate 10 animals. Etaminr ad horses of A177 Bde. Inspect A77 & 1317? Bdes. also 48th M.G. Coy, park horses of 48th Inf. Bde.	O.H
	16.8.16	a.m.	Inspect camp of incipient Kingsmen 112 of Div. Amb. very slight.	O.H

WAR DIARY or INTELLIGENCE SUMMARY

Army Form C. 2118.

A.D.V.S. 16th Div.

Place	Date	Hour	Summary of Events and Information	Remarks and references to Appendices
NOEUX-LES-MINES	17.8.16	am	Inspect 16th Div. Signal Coy. Inspect 144 Bgde AC - Excellent. Judge showing of the 4 Coys of Div. Train. 47 M.V.S. Inocmts 8 animals.	JCA
	18.8.16	am	Inspect A.T.P. — C.11 Bgde & D.17 Bgde. Interview O.C. 177 Bgde re losing of his entraps.	JCA
	19.8.16	am	Conference V.O.S. Inter. hospital examination of skin & eczema.	JCA
	20.8.16	am	Inspect 111th Hants & 47th Inf Bgde. Examine D.H.Q. horses.	
	21.8.16	am	With D.A.D.V.S. round artillery wagon lines to see an outbreak of new cord. Inspect to bd standing for units inspect all units at MAZINGARBE, also 253 Tunnelling Coy. Examine horses of D.180, going 5 undoubted mange cases.	JCA
	22.8.16	8am	47 M.V.S. — 47 mits wounded 8 animals. 47 M.V.S. Inocmts 3 animals by Coy from BETHUNE	JCA
12 noon			See horse loads. Paint St. Rescue to rl. station, examine sorting drawing. Report re mange in civilian horses sent to AA & Q of Army.	JCA
	23.9.16	am	47 Insp. mange 5 more cases by rail. Visit artillery wagon lines & Inf. transport lines, all units mobile. from B. Bgde DDR 1st Army calls re move of Division & reorganisation & Arteries	JCA

Army Form C. 2118.

WAR DIARY
or
INTELLIGENCE SUMMARY.
(Erase heading not required.)

A.D.V.S.
16th Div.

Place	Date	Hour	Summary of Events and Information	Remarks and references to Appendices
NOEUX -LES- -MINES.	24.8.16	am	Visit Div. C. Train & D.A.C.	
			Visit N.Z.I. Remt. Station. BONNEHEM. Finds billet for M.V.S. at ECCEDECQUES. Call to our D.V.S. 1st Army.	OA
			4/M.V.S. evacuate 6 animals by trains from BETHUNE.	
	25.8.16	6.30 pm	Conference of V.O's in reorganisation of Artillery & Infantry on subject. Veterinary personnel and horses. Telephone	OA
		am	Inspected animals of D.W.B. Coln 4/M.V.S. Tomorrow at same Showers, Yards men sick from 15-M.V.S. (8th Div.) to take our stables & stores from 4/Divn.	
		3 pm	Conference of V.O's - 4/M.V.S. evacuate to 16 animals.	OA
RAIMBERT	26.8.16	8 am	4/M.V.S. marched out.	
		10 am	Leave by car Cate at ALLOUAGNE YAUCHEL	
		12.30 pm	Arrive with Div.H.Q. - M.V.S. billets at ECCEDECQUES.	
		3 pm	Visit horses at ECCEDECQUES, & ALLOUAGNE. Hand over 4 surplus animals to R.A. artillery to D.V.S. 1st Army.	OA
	27.8.16	7.30 am	To ECCEDECQUES. Inspects wheelers & gun with staff Capt	OA
			R.A. re reorganisation; visits AMES 4/I.B.F.G.	
	28.8.16	am	Call at R.A. Hd. Qrs. ECCEDECQUES, - only 20 surplus horses from Art. 9/12. from tram transferred to 16 Div.	OA
			Visit M.V.S. & Call Horse D. Div. 1st Army.	
CHOCQUES	29.8.16	11.30 am	Train.	OA
		3.30 pm	Enters with M.O. for the Divisior. 6 animals evacuated by B. & Bn. & M.V.S. Please to Bright off sick to cxy artillery at NOEUX. After M.V.S. to left.	

Army Form C. 2118.

WAR DIARY
or
INTELLIGENCE SUMMARY.
(Erase heading not required.)

A.D.V.S.
16th Divn.

(6)

Place	Date	Hour	Summary of Events and Information	Remarks and references to Appendices
LONGEAU.	30.9.16	12.45am	Britain. Arrive.	
CORBIE.		2.45am	Arrive.	
		11am	Visit all units to Billets in town.	
			D.D.V.S. IV Army called re veterinary arrangements in forward area.	
		4pm	47th V.S. evacuated 16 animals from LILLERS station, returned there with H.Q. 9 for 16th D.A.C. Train by road.	O.K.
F.2.b. (ALBERT Embankment)	31.9.16	10 am	Arrive.	
		11.30am	Proceed to VECQUEMONT, & visit artillery units, 47 mm.s arrived there at 4.30pm, after delay straying row was	O.K.
		12 noon	Several cases of Sarcoptic mange have occurred during the month, the majority in ammunition sub. section, & thorough disinfection, apparent to have checked further spreading of the disease. D.180.v.3.9z. Evacuation of affected animals to have	

C. Stevenson
Major A.V.C.
a.D.V.S. 16th Divn.

WAR DIARY

A.D.V.S. 16th Division

FOR MONTH OF SEPTEMBER, 1916.

VOLUME 10

WAR DIARY or INTELLIGENCE SUMMARY

Army Form C. 2118.

A.D.V.S.
16th Div.

(1)

Place	Date	Hour	Summary of Events and Information	Remarks and references to Appendices
FORK TREE. (Albert L.26.b.9.)	1.9.16	am	Inspected sick of 49th & 47th Inf. Bdes. at HAPPY VALLEY & CITADEL respectively.	
		pm	With O.C. Train inspected watering supply & troughs. Surveyed area. Saw Capt. HOWE A.V.C. to 49 Tn. V.S. to take over duty to form ADVANCED SECTION. Veterinary charge of 77th Bde. R.F.A. Transferred to Capt. LUCKING A.V.C.	OK
	2.9.16	am	Visited 47th & 49th Bde. T.M. Coys. & inspected all sick animals. Visited 180th Bde. R.F.A. & saw Capt. REID A.V.C. in reference to instructions re return of army watering at usual times. Was in HAPPY VALLEY. Water supply good, though mules were trough to a trough. No 2 sub. Divs. in place.	
		pm	Order 4) M.V.S. to withdraw from VECQUEMONT to MORLANCOURT tomorrow.	OK
	3.9.16	am	Saw sick of Signal Coy. & visited Section of D.A.C. which moved up to HAPPY VALLEY.	
		pm	4) M.V.S. arrived & Mr???? from?? MORLANCOURT. Visited & arranged re Advanced Section. M.V.S. landed much 3 horses to relieving section at VECQUEMONT, leaving two men behind for 24 hours.	
	4.9.16	am	Visited saw sick of, 48, 49th Bdes. moved BILLON FARM. Capt. HOWE A.V.C. with Advanced Section went to water Troughs at F.21.b. & Thomas. Horse Ambulance arrived with this train.	OK

WAR DIARY or INTELLIGENCE SUMMARY

Army Form C. 2118.

A.D.V.S. 16th Div.

Place	Date	Hour	Summary of Events and Information	Remarks and references to Appendices
FORK TREE.	4.9.16	pm	Visit M.V.S. at MORLANCOURT. With O.C. M.V.S. visit GROVE TOWN railhead & arrange with R.T.O. to return sick there.	JoA
		5 pm	Interview A.D.V.S. 24th Div.	
		6 pm	Interview A.D.V.S. 20th Div. 16th Div. evacuating sick thence. 16th Div. evacuate to 36. M.V.S.	
CITADEL (F.21.b)	5.9.16	7.30 am	Leave camp.	
		8 am	Arrive, taking over from A.D.V.S. 20th Div. Visit Adv. Sn Station also 177th & 180th F.Bds.	
	6.9.16	pm	Visit 47 M.V.S. - MORLANCOURT.	
		9 am	own horse 16th Div. evacuate to No. 12 M.V.S. & to No. 32 M.V.S.	JoA
		pm	Visit O.C. 47 M.V.S. at FORK TREE, took kit up for him	
		4 pm	M.V.S. moves to FORK TREE, arriving 10 pm	
	7.9.16	am	Move with 2 Echelon D.H.Q. to camp & establish vacated by 5th Div. & 8th Bn. took over veterinary arrangements of 24th Div. & Artillery -BOIS DES TAILLES, from A.D.V.S. 3rd Div.	JoA
		pm	Visit Adv. Sn Station. (6 sows many sick evacuated.) Surveying the cart 24 horses.	
	8.9.16	am	Visit 47 M.V.S. at FORK TREE, 316th F.D.A.C. - HAPPY VALLEY	
		2 pm	Conference of V.Os Sup.P. mule V.O.s of 24th Div. & Artillery to thrash all & late for armies Ch.Hops? sup.P. supply animals of 172th & 180th Bde. a CARNOY - constantly	JoA
		5 pm	interviewed. 47 M.V.S. evacuate 16 cases.	
	9.9.16	am	Visit 47 M.V.S. - FORK TREE, took vet. party t/o Capt House conform section.	JoA

WAR DIARY or INTELLIGENCE SUMMARY

A.D.V.S.
16th Divn.

Army Form C. 2118.

Place	Date	Hour	Summary of Events and Information	Remarks and references to Appendices
CITADEL	9.9.16	4 pm	Inspected vet & walker leg of A.V.C. 108th Bde. 24th Divn — most of the horses require to worming. Sent instrns to replace to A.D.V.S. 24th Divn.	
		6 pm	Inspected Horses of 77th Bde. at CARNOY — Horses of our Battery showing signs of exhaustion & debility — daily average of 47 mus. evacuated. 15 animals from Bn. 26 from 24th Bn. entraining at GROVE TOWN — four horses sent to 11th of CA	
	10.9.16	am	LONDON M.V.S. Visit 47 M.V.S. & inspect all evacuating camps & arrange for inspect all sick of Divl. Train at GROVETOWN (camps were of base standard.)	
		from	Infantry no A.D.V.S. 50th Divn. who taken over vet & admin duties of 24th & 16th Divl. Artillery. Notify V.O.S. accordingly 4 mus. evacd. 13 cars from 16th Bde & 3 from 24th Bn. Return to horses camps — 2nd Echelon D.H.Q. being reinx by Guards Div.	
CORBIE	11.9.16	10.30 am	Arrive. Orders M.V.S. to remain FORK TREE until Corbie	
		11.30 am	47 M.V.S. evacd. 12 animals.	
	12.9.16	am	Inspect animals of H.Q. 7th Irish Rifles, 1st Hemir Lrs 16th Cay. R'd. 145 Cay A.O.C. & 48 M.G. Coy.	
			47 M.V.S. move to SAILLY-LE-SEC.	
		from	Inspect animals of Trench Mor. 143 Cay A.O.C. & trans Mr.S.	

Army Form C. 2118.

WAR DIARY
or
INTELLIGENCE SUMMARY.
(Erase heading not required.)

A.D.V.S.
16th Div.

(4)

Place	Date	Hour	Summary of Events and Information	Remarks and references to Appendices
CORBIE	13.9.16	a.m.	Inspected S.A.A.T. Grand Sect. of D.A.C. - 8th & 49th Dublin Fus: & 11th Hants. Obtained 30,000 rounds of anti-tetanus serum from 21st C.C.S.	from 21st C.C.S.
			too been hunt of Reserve of D.H.Q. — Dept. of 15,000 rounds intra-venously & received large draft of serum sent to our Amm. Column. Suppose a few Locus Saddles.	
	14.9.16		Visited all units of 48th, 49th & 13th Infantry Brigades. Good state of Horses at 7th R'l. Irish & two very bad, and bots of Guns to well horses throughout.	f/olt
	15.9.16	a.m.	At Divl Conference of A.D's & V.S at IV Army H.Q. Inspected D.H.Q horses & 11½ F.A Brown Bn'y at 7th Irish Rifles & 12½ hrs res two	f/olt
			to 4) M.V.S. at SAILLY-LE-SEC. Lines put care for use in following day —	f/olt
	16.9.16		4) M.V.S. moved its lines to from MERICOURT	
	17.9.16	a.m.	to SAILLY-LE-SEC. Inspected M.V.S. horses at 12.30pm. at LA CHAUSSEE, & billets for their use.	f/olt
			4) M.V.S. moved for Animal Co. march to CORBIE, en route to	f/olt
			Visited all units at CORBIE.	
HALLEN-COURT	18.9.16	8 am Leave arriv.	47 Divl march BAIRAINNES & thence billets	f/olt

Army Form C. 2118.

WAR DIARY
or
INTELLIGENCE SUMMARY.
(Erase heading not required.)

A.D.V.S. 16th Divn.

Place	Date	Hour	Summary of Events and Information	Remarks and references to Appendices
HALLENCOURT	19.9.16	a.m.	Visit unit at ALLERY & AIRAINES. See sick of 155 Coy. A.S.C. & H.Q. 48th Bde.	
		p.m.	to ABBEVILLE. Arrange to grant 36 Remounts from the Remount Squadron from No 2 Adv Remount Squadron. Interview O.C. N° 22 B.V.H. who will arrange to send to AIRAINES. for all sick left behind by 47 M.V.S.	J.B.A.
	20.9.16	a.m.	Inspected animals to no. of 36 animals from N° 2 Adv Rmt Sqn and litter at AIRAINES.	J.B.A.
		p.m.	Visit 47 M.V.S. Arrange to have sick collected with visit units at LIMEUX & HUPPY.	J.B.A.
BAILLEUL	21.9.16	7 a.m.	Leave, & entrain at PONT REMY at 9.30 a.m.	
		6.30 p.m.	Detrain.	
WESTOUTRE (Belgium Sheet 28SW 9.c.)		8 p.m.	Arrive & billet.	
	22.9.16	a.m.	M.V.S. entrains LONGPRÉ (Somme) annexed to A/RAINING Coy. to collection by N° 22. B.V.H. M.V.S. detrain GODEWAERSVELDE & march to MEULENBEUCK. billeting at farm at 5.2.a.8.8 (Belgium Sheet 28.SW.)	J.B.A.
		p.m.	Visit 4th Canadian M.V.S. at MISDS. 3.3. & arrange re 47.M.V.S. taking over, in their absence.	J.B.A.
	23.9.16	a.m.	Visits Rendezvous at 49 Bde, 114 Hours to 155 & 156 Coys R.E. Interview with A.D.V.S. 2 Army, & arrangements made to hand to British command up of the Bn — a large number of badly caparisoned Algerian &	J.B.A.

2353 W. W3541/1454 700,000 5/15 D. D. & L. A.D.S.S./Forms/C. 2118.

WAR DIARY / INTELLIGENCE SUMMARY

Army Form C. 2118.

A.D.V.S. 16th Div.

Place	Date	Hour	Summary of Events and Information	Remarks and references to Appendices
WEST-OUTRE	24.9.16	am	Visit proposed new site for M.V.S. - convenient water + accommodation in ST GRUELT, so arrange to take over site vacated by 4th Canadian M.V.S. tomorrow.	O/R
	25.9.16	am	With D.A.Q.M.G. visit all transport lines in Bn. & also inspect 143, 144 + 145 Coys. A.S.C.	
		pm	Inspect and arrange all transport of 49th Inf. Bde. 2nd Canadian Lancashire Regt. 260 & forage transport of Army Service Corps. also Divisional Train in civilian horses + also a V.O.C.R.E. Owners wishing to that this camp & to re-attend D.D.V.S. 2nd Army & also to that this camp of Belgian authority, took place so far as came in range of Canadians.	O/R
	26.9.16	am	With D.A.Q.M.G. + V.S. [?] Capt[?] 3rd Canadian Artillery inspect animals of 41st, 46th, 33rd, 44th, 39th & 38th Batteries C.F.A. & Nos. 1, 2, 3 H.T. Sections D.A.C. B + left on a few cases of debilitating & [?] horses & a few isolated cases of DEBILITY camp influencing [?] the latter.	
		pm	Inspected horses all transport of 47th Inf. Bde. + M.G. Coys + 47th H.V.S. visit on to 7 annexed by spinal sick transport Transport V.O. of 3rd Canadian Artillery	WIPPENHOCK
	27.9.16	am	Inspect all DEBILITY sick from 3rd Canadian Artillery at 47th Hrs. admit 50 [?]	
		pm	Inspect transport of 48th Bde. & m.g. Coy on parade.	O/R

2353 Wt. W2544/1454 700,000 5/15 D.D. & L. A.D.S.S./Forms/C. 2118.

Army Form C. 2118.

WAR DIARY
or
INTELLIGENCE SUMMARY.
(Erase heading not required.)

A.D.V.S.
16th Div.

Place	Date	Hour	Summary of Events and Information	Remarks and references to Appendices
WEST-OUTRE.	28.9.16	am / pm	Wrote O.C. 47 M.V.S. Select animals for evacuation. Inspect 113th Fd. Amb. Twenty mules sent from 3 Div to training at M.V.S.	JA
	29.9.16	am	D.D.V.S. 2nd Army surfaces to animals for evacuation at M.V.S. 59 animals evacuated by road to St OMER. 1st up at N°5 — Sick Horse Hosl, & 2nd up at N°2. S.H.H.	JA
		2.30 pm / 4.30 pm	Conference of V.Os with D.D.V.S. at N°5–S.H.H. BORRE, & to see sick animals & pickets, &c.	
	30.9.16	am / pm	Conference of A.D.V.S. at BAILLEUL. Visit M.M.P. horses LOCRE, & 7th Divn. two.	JA
			While in 4th Army area on SOMME, 47 M.V.S. admitted 112 animals from this & other Divisions, 110 of which were evacuated. Transport animals to remount trains this section, while in 4th Army area with the exception of 1 at remount to & 7 sent to 2 were sent to suffered through want of proper care & feeding	

J. Robinson
Major
A.D.V.S. 16th Div.

WAR DIARY

MONTH OF OCTOBER, 1916.

VOLUME No. 11

A.D.V.S. 16th Division

WAR DIARY / INTELLIGENCE SUMMARY

Army Form C. 2118.

A.D.V.S.
16th Div.

Place	Date	Hour	Summary of Events and Information	Remarks and references to Appendices
WEST-OUTRE	5.10.16	a.m.	D.D.V.S. 2nd Army called. Visit 47th V.S. Inspect 11th Hants (Pioneers) showing cases of SARCOPTIC mange to the V.S. Visit 157 Coy. R.E., 6th Rl. Irish Rif. & 4th M.G. Coy. Troops appear to be watering horses very bad, will be a source of trouble when winter comes.	O.A.
	6.10.16	a.m.	Inspect 7th Leinster Rifs. watering arrangements for 7th Inf. Bde. All appear bad. Six horses attached from 11th Hants for building stables. (47th V.S.)	O.A.
	7.10.16	a.m.	Visit V.O. of 16th Divl. Artillery, arrived today at METEREN and visit all horses standings vacated by Canadian Artillery, so horses are reported to have been left behind. Two have been collected by M.V.S. during	O.A.
		3 p.m.	that. 29 Remounts for Dvhns arrived at STEENWERCK STATION.	
		6 p.m.	WH DAQMG. moves remounts to be sent to LOCRE.	O.A.
	8.10.16		Visit Transport Lines of 7th MUNSTER FUS. & 7th IRISH RIFLES, also M.V.S. APs. A 2000 for Artillery arrival - delays important. Draft to be sent to D.D.V.S.	O.A.
	9.10.16	a.m.	Visit H.Q. & 142 Coy. Divl. Train. Arrange for watering places. 77th Bde R.F.A.	O.A.
		p.m.	Divl. Artillery move into 'Ow' AREA.	
	10.10.16	a.m.	Visit 47th M.V.S.	O.A.
		a.m.	With D.D.V.S. inspect 77th Bde. R.F.A. & 16th D.A.C.) A large number of DEBILITY	
			177th Bde. & 180th Bde R.F.A.) cases now vacated.	
	11.10.16	a.m.	Inspect cases of debilitated animals of divisional artillery from 180 Bde. & 77 Bde.	O.A.
		p.m.	Phone for vacation 180 Bde = 99. 77th = 17. 177 = 39 D.A.C. = 26 also HQ Div. Trn RD Train. Sewered D.V.S. immediately. Visit 7. V.S.	
	12.10.16	a.m.	Visit C. 180 Bde. re unfit V.O. re evacuation of sick remainder. Visit to V.S. Inspect 142 Coy. A.D.C. with O.C. Train, also unfit him & unfit REMT. OFFICER N.6 Area, re turn of horses.	
		2.30 p.m.	Conference of V.Os. re infect of tf vaccine. of 147 animals by shrapnel fire. Tomorrow V.Os. to take them in own sick to be marked W, POPERINGHE 8 a.m. Capt. HOWE A.V.C. will be O.C. Train. Arrange with Staff Capt. R.A.	O.A.

HOWE AVC. WIll be OC Train arrange with staff capt R.A.

Army Form C. 2118.

WAR DIARY
or
INTELLIGENCE SUMMARY.
(Erase heading not required.)

A.D.V.S. 16th Div.

Place	Date	Hour	Summary of Events and Information	Remarks and references to Appendices
WEST-OUTRE	13.10.16	8 am	Sapeurs entraining of 203 animals from the three Divisions, at WIPPENHOEK SIDING. Train delayed owing to 3. M.V.S. arriving late. Capt. HOWE AVC to train.	J.A.
		11.30 am	Visit wagon lines 7th & 8th Field Amb.	
		from	Conference of V.Os. with M.V.S. Army instructions re entraining of BAILLEUL and visit of 116 training point 77th & 177th Bde. R.F.A.	
	14.10.16 to 25.10.16		No special news. 116 animals evac to 15.10.16	
	26.10.16	am	Inspect all wagon lines of 180th Bde. R.F.A. attached 23rd Div - also Horse fuelde[?] fair, though a good many exhibits came from behind lines. V.B. -/c- Bde. (Capt. REID A.V.C.) on leave 20.4 to 30.4	
		from	Visit D.A.C. D/177 Bde & Tn. V.S. inspect D/177 Bde. 41 Tn. V.S. evacuates 40 animals.	J.A.
	27.10.16	am	Inspect Transport of 41st Inf. Bde.	
		from	Conference of V.Os. Visit M.V.S.	
	28.10.16	am	With D.D. R.2 & Army inspect horses of 77th Bde. R.F.A. T	J.A.
			Stables standing of D.A.C.	
		from	Inspect Out Signal Coy animals, & B/177 Bde, & looking at details of coys to evacuation	
	29.10.16	am	Inspect A Coy D/177 Bde. reduced debility cases for evac from J.O.H.	J.A.
	30.10.16	am	Inspect 4 A.B.C. D(?) Bde. Bde reduced debility cases for evac too	
		from	Visit H.Q. from M.V.S. Capt. HOWE AVC admit to hospital (I.C.T. face) Capt. LENTON A.V.C. commands convoy of the futures - 3 cornered up the Line Hellfire LOCRE	J.A.

Army Form C. 2118.

WAR DIARY
or
INTELLIGENCE SUMMARY.
(Erase heading not required.)

A.D.V.S.
16th Div.

Place	Date	Hour	Summary of Events and Information	Remarks and references to Appendices
WEST-OUTRE.	31.10.16	11.16 am	Inspected transport of 11th Hants (P), 156 Field Coy. R.E. & 48th Inf. Bde. Inspected 49th Inf. Bde. Transport.	A.D.V.S. 16th Div.
			Most of the animals evacuated from this Division during the month, were suffering from Debility, the majority of the animals having had conformation, the loss of condition to a large extent due to them being overworked in the FOURTH ARMY area, & to insufficient watering on the march. In some parts of the country it was impossible to water horses satisfactorily unless battalions made up parties & to some extent too, the loss of condition may be ascribed to faulty stable-management.	J.S. Andrews Inspector A.D.V.S. 16th Div.

2353 Wt. W2544/1454 700,000 5/15 D.D.&L.   A.D.S.S./Forms/C. 2118.

WAR DIARY.

FOR

MONTH OF NOVEMBER, 1916.

VOLUME 12.

A.D.V.S. 16th Division

WAR DIARY / INTELLIGENCE SUMMARY

Army Form C. 2118.

A.D.V.S. 16th Div.

Place	Date	Hour	Summary of Events and Information	Remarks and references to Appendices
WEST-OUTRE	1.11.16	am	Visit 47 M.V.S.	
		pm	Capt. REID A.V.C. reported having returned from leave. Subscriptions to "Lord Kitchener's National Memorial Fund" from officers, NCOs & men A.V.C. of this Bn. forwarded to D.D.V.S.	D.A
	2.11.16	am	Capt. LENTON A.V.C. proceeded to BOULOGNE for dental treatment. He to return to 10 days leave, on completion of treatment. 9 Cable command of 47 M.V.S. during his absence.	D.A
		11am	D.D.R. 2nd Army inspects "Renovall" carriage at M.V.S.	
	3.11.16		Attended Action re ward at M.V.S.	D.A
		am	to 47 M.V.S. Inspect 157 Coy R.E. + 250 Tunnelling Coy. Embark 11 animals from 47 M.V.S.	
		pm	Visit 2 from Lieutenant A.D.V.S. 36th Div at 47 M.V.S.	D.A
	4.11.16	am	Inspect 157 Coy R.E. & H.Q. 48th Inf. Bde. Capt. REID A.V.C. (188 H.A.F.A.) reports for duty from 29th Div. Proceeds to H.Q. 49th Inf. Bde. & takes over Capt HOWE's charge from Capt McMAHON.	D.A
		pm	To 2nd ARMY Sv. to Remount Section to inspect 7 Remounts received. Inlieving D.D.V.S. 2nd ARMY H.Q.	D.A
	5.11.16	am	to 47 M.V.S.	D.A
	6.11.16	am	Inspect Transport of 4th P. 49th Inf. Bde. 48th & 49th M.G. Coys. 7113th & 4th Auxiliary.	D.A
		pm	at 47 M.V.S.	
	7.11.16	am	at 47 M.V.S. ALC Coy T.A.V.C. parade at my office 9 am	D.A
		pm	Inspect 47, 112th Fd. Amb. Estab for 1st visit A.W.R.A. & M.M.R.	D.A

Army Form C. 2118.

WAR DIARY
or
INTELLIGENCE SUMMARY.
(Erase heading not required.)

A.D.V.S.
16th Div"

Place	Date	Hour	Summary of Events and Information	Remarks and references to Appendices
WEST-OUTRE	15.11.16	a.m.	With Capt. REID investigation outbreak of PSOROPTIC MANGE in 1st Canadian Tunnelling Coy. - 5 hund. cases sent to M.V.S. Inspection & Disinfection carried out. Visit 3 Connaughts & 6 Munsters. Visit 11 Labour Batt" & my part 250 of Lines, Coy, & 1st Brokenshire Inspect Transport of 11 & 9th Ambulance at METEREN (Bkfy Casualty) with R.E. for supply of material for the Laying of 2 smaller evacuation by H.A.S. 150 & H.O. MER. B.V.H.	J.A.
	16.11.16	a.m.	Visit 47 M.V.S. & inspect 1 Leinster's Transport. Inspect M.M. Pts DH.Q. horses on parade. Visit H.Q. Div. & Van.	J.A.
	17.11.16	a.m.	2.047 M.V.S. Inspect Transport of 7 & 8 Innis Fus, 2nd Rgt & 2nd C.Reg, + 7/8 Irish Fus.	J.A.
		p.m.	Conference of V.O.'s. Visit 2 & 7th Dublin Fus. arrived yesterday in METEREN area. Skin Condition - condition fair.	J.A.
	18.11.16	a.m.	Visit 15/17 Bde. on removal of water troughs. Inspect 8 & 9 R. Dub. Fus. 47 Rgt. Irish Rifles & 1st Munster's Transport - Filter carried on in 8th Dublins & others of Regiment in 7 & 8 Rifles. There were all so unclipped horses, the Brigadier refusing to allow any animals of the Brigade to be clipped. Except to remove animals & enlarge in the Trenches. Trenching.	J.A.
	19.11.16	a.m.	Visit 47 M.V.S. & enlarg. intermed. of 198 animals in Free. at WYPENHOER - 19 animals evacuated from this Division - O.C 47 M.V.S. proceeds in charge of Evacuation.	J.A.
		p.m.	at 47 M.V.S.	J.A.

Army Form C. 2118.

WAR DIARY
or
INTELLIGENCE SUMMARY.
(Erase heading not required.)

A.D.V.S
16th Div=

(4)

Place	Date	Hour	Summary of Events and Information	Remarks and references to Appendices
WEST-OUTRE.	20.11.16	am	Inspect 1st Can. Tunnelling Coy; effective measures have been taken to deal with outbreak of PSOROPTIC mange 9 of them, 10 horses have been evacuated. Inspect 156 + 157 Coys. R.E. 11th Hank (P), 6th Rfy & 2nd Rfy + H.Q. & M.G. Coy. 47th Inf. Bde.	J.O.A.
	21.11.16	am	To 47 M.V.S.	J.O.A.
		am	Inspect A.C. + D/117 Bde. Visit deps transports who in showing much to 47 M.V.S. (too solid)	J.O.A.
	22.11.16	am	Inspect A.B.C. + D/117 Bde. Debilitated animals in cattle not improving.	
		pm	To 47 M.V.S. 6 mules detailed from 47 Inf Bde to work mowing machine for camp work.	J.O.A.
	23.11.16	am	Inspect animals of M.M.P. + D.H.Q. Lieut. CAWTHORNE A.V.C. from No 12. B.V.H. reports for duty with this Division. Vice Capt. HOWE A.V.C.	J.O.A.
		pm	Inspect surplus animals at transport lines of 1st Inniskillins. 2nd Rifle Bde. Inspect Debility cases animals & those prepared for casting at 142 Coy A.S.C.	J.O.A.
	24.11.16	am	Inspect & classify 49 surplus animals shown 5th Tunnels. Coy. 2nd Bn Suff. Th. 24 surplus animals herefly yoked to the Division.	J.O.A.
		pm	Conference of VOs. To 47 M.V.S.	J.O.A.
	25.11.16	am	Supervise entrainment of 55 animals from the Division at WIPPENHOEK.	J.O.A.
		12 noon	D.D.R. Wt.W254/1454 700,000 5/15 D.D.&L. & D.S.S. (Forms) C. 2118. Insp. D.D.R. refund to cast 4 enumerable tives. Cases, which were referred to remit, by the on Svin. To 47 M.V.S.	J.O.A.

Army Form C. 2118.

WAR DIARY or INTELLIGENCE SUMMARY.
(Erase heading not required.)

A.D.V.S.
16th Division

Place	Date	Hour	Summary of Events and Information	Remarks and references to Appendices
WEST-OUTRE	26.11.16	11 am	Visit A.D. Gos. Rest Train; went to O.C. in respect some horses of 142 Coy. 2/4 M.V.S.	J.A.
	27.11.16	am	Inspect transport of 4 battalions 49th Inf. Bde. & 113th Fd. Amb. 2/4 M.V.S. Sent warrant to Capt. BROAD A.V.C. proceeding on leave and 29th. Capt. McMAHON, A.V.C. evacuated sick to C.C.S.	J.A.
	28.11.16	am	Interview O/c the Roads. IX Corps. H.Q. Inspect 111th Fd. Amb. by METEREN. Visit Corps Horse Isol. Hosp. Tank in course of construction; about ship 27 x 6. C. 10.0. on BAILLEUL SHAEKKEN road.	J.A.
	29.11.16	am	To 113th Fd. Amb. evacuation to retain a station. Inspect 143, 144 & 145 Coys. A.o.C. - afew cases of lice in 2nd Coy. Interview A.D.V.S. 34th Div. re horse stantion of horses by half from BAC SAN MAUR. Capt. BROAD A.V.C. proceeds on leave.	J.A.
	30.11.16	9 am	Inspect M.M.P. horses.	
		9.30 am	,, ,, of D.H.Q.	J.A.
		10.30 ,,	,, animals to few evacuation at 4/1 M.V.S.	
		12 noon	D/7 Bdr. - great improvement	
		pm	Inspect 1, 2 & 4 Sections 16th D.A.C.	

Remarks:- A few cases of Influenza, Pyrexia & Mange have occurred during the month of November; in most cases been traced to remounts.

Shoeing:- about 1/3 of the animals of the Division are newly shod with the D.V.S. No. 17/4050/16, of 10.11.16). This has not proved satisfactory. the Iron wearing down from a further

J. Andrews
A.D.V.S. 16th Division

WAR DIARY FOR MONTH OF DECEMBER, 1916.

VOLUME 13.

A.D.V.S., 16th Division

Army Form C. 2118.

WAR DIARY
or
INTELLIGENCE SUMMARY.
(Erase heading not required.)

A.D.V.S.
16th Div

Place	Date	Hour	Summary of Events and Information	Remarks and references to Appendices
WESTOUTRE	1.12.16	a.m.	Inspect 136 A.T. Coy. – 1st Can. Tunnelling Coy. – 250th Tunnelling Coy & 11th Labour Coy. – 9 animals evacuated by tpt from BAILLEUL	App up
	2.12.16		Conference of V.Os. 2o/47 M.V.S. – D.D.V.S. called at FIELD A.Q.M.G. transport 96 Remounts at WIPPENHOEK estry	
		9 a.m.	Inspect Div. Supply Coy. transport 2o/47 M.V.S.	
		11 a.m.	Sat. S.S.O. with reference to oats (half transport) remount to C/177 Bde. Wire Friday. – 3 cars of to be on patrol of two Battery cates up Rly.	
	3.12.16	a.m.	Inspect horses bb 2nd Army T.M. School	App A
			Inspect 157th Field Coy. R.E. – 48th & 49th M.G. Coys. – Vinde 47 M.V.S. officer	
	4.12.16	a.m.	Inspect A, B, & C/177th Bde & D/177 Bde – tenues improving. Latrines still bad. Oats now being served in 112 lb sacks are of inferior quality – mules quiet.	App A
			2o/47 M.V.S. – 500 concrete slabs (2ft. sqrs) many mustily kept	
			12 animals evac to by road to STOMER	
	5.12.16	a.m.	Inspect A. & D/177 Bde. – D Battery still bad. – Exp. animal of forage being. weigh Ea	
			F.O.C. Train inspect heavy draught wagons horses	App A
			180th Bde R.F.A. (ordered to 47th Div.)	
			to BERTHEN Foundering in breaking up of horses kept up	
	6.12.16	a.m.	to MALIN 177 Bde account of steps of tension there	App A

WAR DIARY or INTELLIGENCE SUMMARY

Army Form C. 2118.

A.D.V.S. 16th Div.

Place	Date	Hour	Summary of Events and Information	Remarks and references to Appendices
WEST-OUTRE	27.12.16	a.m.	Visit H.Q. 16th D.A.C. & interview C.O. Visit 13th D. Batteries 177 Bde. re inspection of stables & harness of A.T.H.H.H. Bde. re transport & watering arrangements. Visit H.Q. 16th Div. Train.	O.A.
	28.12.16	a.m.	Inspect A.T.B. Batteries 177/Bde. & select sick & lame horses for evacuation from latter. 180th Bde. R.F.A. rejoins Division.	O.A.
		p.m.	To 47 M.V.S.	
	29.12.16	a.m.	Inspect transport of 112th Inf. Ambulance & to 47 M.V.S. Conference at V.O.S. Visit H.Q. 47th & 49th Inf. Bde. Report on horsing with unfit staff horses sent to D.A.T.O.	O.A.
		p.m.	M.V.S. Evacuate two journeys to by barges from BAC SAN MAUR.	
	30.12.16	a.m.	Inspect 142 Coy. A.S.C. with F.H.O.E. Train, Folkstone address is proposed to Brigade. Check A.B.64 of all Supply/S.A.V.C. in Div. Visit M.V.S. Inspect animals at Div. School.	O.A.
		p.m.	Inspect all animals of 180 Inf. Bde. in waggon lines, Highway seafront to MANGE cases. Horses in whole, ... still fair. A few Div. sick & camps for evacuation.	O.A.
	31.12.16	a.m.	To 47 M.V.S.	
			APHTHA CONTAGIOSA. - 49 cases during last fortnight, confined to 4 Batteries & two in all cases to be taken on equipment by Remounts. P.U.N. - Considered by half our shoeing & farriers total, commenced two weeks ago. Percentage of casts tender (not annual at height.) During November Div. 242. December 113. Very little lameness on march from the departure of shoeing.	

J. Ackl. Tugumo
A.D.V.S. 16th Div.

WAR DIARY for month of JANUARY, 1917.

VOLUME 14

A.D.V.S. 16th Division

Army Form C. 2118.

WAR DIARY
or
INTELLIGENCE SUMMARY.
(Erase heading not required.)

A.D.V.S.
16th Div.

Place	Date	Hour	Summary of Events and Information	Remarks and references to Appendices
WEST-OUTRE	JANUARY 1917. 8th	a.m.	Interview Brigadier - 48th Inf Bde, re that Brigade.	G.A
	9th		Interview A.D.V.S. 41st Div. - Office	
		7 a.m.	Inspect all horses of Divisional Train at Refilling Point	WIPPENHOEK
		10.30 a.m.	Office.	G.A
	10th	p.m a.m.	Inspect horses of 180th Bde. - Inspect cars of horses in B.M.O. for A. with A.D.V.S. 41st Div. to inspect animals at shelters.	
		p.m.	34 Reinforcements arrive HOPOUTRE. Capt. LENTON to inspect them.	G.A
	11th	a.m 9.30 10.30	Inspect D.H.Q. horses 54 Remounts at D.A.C. lines No 2 & 3 Sections D.A.C.	G.A
		11 a.m		
	12th	a.m.	20 & 47 M.V.S. evacuate 22 animals by road to STOMER	
	13th	a.m	Conference of V. Os. - Office. Examination of all holders of 180 & 180 B.St. for Mange - Selected/every Off. - 14 suspicious. - 14 slightly suspicious. Visited A/180 B.St. Arrange for suspects to remain & come to to stables at M17 b 2.3 tomorrow.	G.A
	14th	p.m. a.m.	Office. examination of skin scrapings. Examine all horses A Bt & C/180 B.St for mange. - B.T.C.-chang. D/180 B.St - clean.	G.A
	15th	p.m. a.m.	Visit C/180 B.St. & 47 M.V.S. - 36 animals evacuated by road VOORMANGE. Interview D.D.V.S. at 2nd Army HQ. Conference of V.Os. w	G.A

Army Form C. 2118.

WAR DIARY
or
INTELLIGENCE SUMMARY.

A.D.V.S. 16th Div.

Place	Date	Hour	Summary of Events and Information	Remarks and references to Appendices
WEST-OUTRE	JANUARY			
	23rd	am	With D.A.P.M.O. inspect all animals to 47th Inf. Bde., also to BARDE MANGE cars at 49th Dublin Fus., M.V.S. siemens F gunners to BARDE ADVS. 36th Bde in METEREN. Interview OA	
		pm	Inspect transport of 111th Inf. Bde to Amb. METEREN. Interview OA ADVS. 36th Bde in MANGE	
	24th	am	Examine all animals to 9th Dublin Fus. to MANGE. Inspect supplies cars of 7th Irish Rifles, 7/8th Innisk Fus, & 2nd Inf. Ryl. Irish Regt. Inspect all MANGE transport cars, A.B.& D/180 Bde. D/177 Bde OA	
		pm	At & D/177 Bde. Visit 142 Coy. A.V.C.	
	25th	am	Inspect D.H.Q. & M.M.T. horses. Visit H.Q. 16th D.A.C. Inspect OA Inspected MANGE cars of 7th Innisk Fus. M.V.S. officer	
		pm	to 47 M.V.S. C.D. & MANGE cars by car to St. OMER.	
	26th	am	Inspect supplies MANGE cars at B/177 Bde & H.Q. & 49th Inf. Bde OA Conference of V.O.s to 47 MVS. Construction of reservable kits	
		pm	to 47 Bde. 23. B.V.H. St. OMER, to inspect MANGE cars was ordered OA	
	27th	am	from the Division accordingly	
	28th	am	Inspect MANGE transport at Inf. transport cars. 47 MVS OA at 142 Coy. A.V.C.	
	29th	am	Inspect transport inspected at A.B.& D/180/132 ... OA Interview ADVS 36th Div. in Lakingarn Conference Dep OA event D.Drs. called	
	6.30pm		D.Drs. called, re employ numerous Wrabbing MV. Orders re detail for IX Corps Horse Dep and 31 Bt, next in ... D.A.P.M.G	

Army Form C. 2118.

WAR DIARY
or
INTELLIGENCE SUMMARY.
(Erase heading not required.)

A.D.V.S.
16th Division

Place	Date	Hour	Summary of Events and Information	Remarks and references to Appendices
WEST-OUTRE	JANUARY 30th	am	Visit to 47 M.V.S. & A/177th Bde.	
		pm	Office. Inspected Capt. LUCKING, A.V.C. in Dept. in charge of Inspectables of B/180 Bde., which are being slaughtered by M.V.S.	
	31st	am	Saw. Visit was a continuation of D/180 Bde. & D/17 Bde. Saw one advance section of IX Corps Horse Dept from A.D.V.S. 26th Dw during his absence on leave. Capt. LUCKING, A.V.C. in Fales on duty at "Dip" his 1st day. B/180 Bde (119 horses) put through the "Dip" with all equipment, from 7.30 am to 12.30 pm. Visit "Dip" which is working well — all may & suspected cases & Divn (109 animals) within have frequent put off through "Dip" from 1.30pm to 4.30pm.	
			STOMATITIS CONTAGIOSA. — 570 cases and 10 treatment at beginning of month. No new cases, & no new running now. Ordered to form a Laboratory. Introduced by removing to Ready. Guard to exhibit, treatment. Thoroughly preventing of inoculable & uninfected takes Period of incubation appears to be about 10 to 14 days. In majority of cases serious complications to tongue, the mucous membrane of which was infiltrated. Dr. in own 1 cases.	
			SARCOPTIC MANGE. — An outbreak in 180th Bde. R.F.A. which recently rejoined Division. Isolation camp in another unit. Very few fresh cases in other depots appear to have been averted.	

D. Rutherford
Major
A.D.V.S. 16th Divn

WAR DIARY.

FOR MONTH OF FEBRUARY, 1917.

VOLUME 15

UNIT:- A.D.V.S. 16th Division

WAR DIARY
or
INTELLIGENCE SUMMARY
(Erase heading not required.)

Army Form C. 2118.

A.D.V.S. 16th Division

Place	Date	Hour	Summary of Events and Information	Remarks and references to Appendices
WEST-OUTRE.	1.2.17	a.m.	Inspected M.M.P. & D.H.Q. horses - also 1st Can. Tunnelling Coy. 11th Hants (P) & 156 & 157 Field Corps R.E.	/out
	2.2.17	p.m. a.m. p.m.	To 47 M.V.S. To IX Corps Horse Dep. & on to IX Corps 'Q'. Interview D.A.Q.M.G. IX Corps arranging for MS to meet weekly, visiting on alternate Suns. Recommended for extension of working hours of Dep. exhibition to IX Corps - copy to D. Dep. S. for information.	
	3.2.17	a.m. p.m.	Inspected A.B.C & D/171 Bde Feld Ambulance - very unsympathetic. To 47 M.V.S.	/out
	4.2.17	a.m.	With D.A.Q.M.G. to WITTENHOEK to meet Remounts - train late, wait around for field of Ennoon. Visit IX Corps Horse Dep.	
		3 p.m 5 p.m	Inspected IX Corps "Dep" after busy inspection. Endeavour to trace away from the place in few weeks. Placed new Co. than to get 2 inch. Interview "Q" & S.O. R.E. IX Corps re repairs. Rec. officers & Dep - arrange to complete repair by 17th. Rept. officers & Dep. - arrange to complete repair by 17th. while the horse be in field CCB. Repairs completed by 11 pm.	/out
	5.2.17	a.m. p.m.	Other With O.C. train inspect train horses attached 77 M.B.S. & 2a (Army Artillery) at POPERINGHE.	/out
	6.2.17 7.2.17		Sick. 300 animals from Division put through Corps Horse Dep.	/out

WAR DIARY / INTELLIGENCE SUMMARY

Army Form C. 2118.

A.D.V.S. 16th Div.

Place	Date	Hour	Summary of Events and Information	Remarks and references to Appendices
WEST-OUTRE	19.2.17	9 am	After inspection of same before going to canteen by D.D.R. Visit 144 Coy. A.S.C. & inspect sick cars. Interview C.R.A. re clipping of horses, specially with regard to C/177 Bde	
		pm	Call & Div. to report re Canteen Vouchers, also Cpls Q & O. See Corps photos.	
	20.2.17	am	Inspect MANGE trainees cases at 177 B.A.C., also D/177 Bde. Visit 47 M.V.S.	OH
			Office	
	21.2.17	am	Inspect all horses of D/177 Bde ovens franes, the battery being drawn up under my observation for scheme. Visit D/177 mayo lines, stables by inspected by mrs.	
		pm	Sanitary Squad	
		5 pm	To HQ 70 Div re E.L.D.A.Q.M.G. & to see 40 Revs. re	OH
	22.2.17	am	Inspect 40 Revs. to remove to Division. Visit Corps Horse info & S.O.R.E. 1A Corps ? on pm to Div	
		pm	20 47 M.V.S.	OH
	23.2.17	am	Inspect horses for canteen at 142 Coy & remount to see 142 Coy. A.S.C. also two cases of MANGE in civilian mules at MONT DES CATS.	
		pm	Conference of V.O.s. Visit & D.V.S. at Corps Horse info Visit Corps Q re proposed form sifo.	OH

Army Form C. 2118.

WAR DIARY or INTELLIGENCE SUMMARY

(Erase heading not required.)

A.D.V.S.
16th Div.

Place	Date	Hour	Summary of Events and Information	Remarks and references to Appendices
WEST-OUTRE	24.2.17	a.m.	Inspect M.A.N.G.E. & mange pits & camp of C/177 Bde. (Capt A/172 Bde, 36th Div) at D RANOUTRE; also camp of 2nd Can. Tunnel Coy.	
			Inspect skin camp at D/177 Bde & visit B/177 Bde. R.F.A.	off
		p.m.	20.4) M.V.S.	
	25.2.17	a.m.	Inspect remounts of 16th Div. train	off
		p.m.	Inspect horses of 180th Bde. R.F.A. Veterinary Enquiry Officer	
	26.2.17	a.m.	To Corps Horse life. Had our own charge of B/o A.D.V.S. 36th Division, and held return home exam.	off
		p.m.	With O.C. Brigade inspect horses of C/180 Bde - 60 Beh. by carbs — 16 for evacuation; also mange of B/180 Bde	off
			20.4) M.V.S.	
	27.2.17	a.m.	Visit 14th Coy A.S.C. & D/177 Bde. Inspect sy Cy. & Range	off
		p.m.	Suspected carrs of A/177 Bde	
			20.4) M.V.S.	
	28.2.17	a.m.		
		p.m.	MANGE.- has more or less been kept under control in the Division, but the number of cases of mange admitted to have been running in excess by the regiment of 177 & A.F.A. Bde. in this area, over say a week, been showed the hoph. Div. at Corp. Horse life, but that the horses of the unit to form after their clate has and pun 1 February 1/60 per day are affected.	

2449 Wt: W4957/M09 750,000 1/16 J.B.C. & A. Forms/C.2118/12.

WAR DIARY
FOR MONTH OF MARCH, 1917.

VOLUME 16

UNIT:- A.D.V.S. 16th Division

Army Form C. 2118.

WAR DIARY
or
INTELLIGENCE SUMMARY

(Erase heading not required.)

A.D.V.S.
16th Div.

Place	Date 1917 MARCH	Hour	Summary of Events and Information	Remarks and references to Appendices
WEST-OUTRE	1st	am	Inspection of H.H.P. & D.H.Q. of 16th Div. Visit & inspection of 77th B.A.C. & IX Corps Horse Disp. Annexe of 77th B.A.C. & 1/180 Bde R.F.A. Being inspected, also all MANGE suspects cases of the Division.	OA
	2nd	from am	Inspect 136 A.T. Coy, 250th Tunnelling Coy., 2nd Can. Siege 2 Coy, 21st Entrenching Bn. Visit 11th Fd. Amb. to receive annexe to note to find MANGE & Ringworm.	OA
	3rd	from am	Visit 112th Fd. & Amb. & saw MANGE case. Conference of V.O.'s. Inspect transport of H.Q. 49th Bde & 7 M.B. Coy 7/8 Duke two. 7/8 Innisk two & 1/3rd ftrs & ambulance. See sick horses at D.H.Q. & 47 M.V.S.	OA
	4th	from am	Visit 1/17th Bde where a new & urgent case to report to also STOMATITIS. These are case of this disease. 47 M.V.S. evacuated 2 horses to ST OMER by motor ambulance officer.	OA
	5th	am from am	Wharfdale Regt Hy transport evacuated 48th & 2nd & 13th to 47 M.V.S. – 32 animals evacuated by road to ST OMER sent to regiment for truck. Was too ill to walk. Lines to which many buy stables, out & travels by rain. SATURDAY MONDAY. It will be seen from copy herd D.I.D on duty	OA
	6th	am from am	Visit sick two of D.A.C. & find cases of infected MANGE Inspect 65th & 1/130th R.A. D.S. & Ambo. Diff. & Infbr Sig Troop into polygonal annexes of 111th F.A. & parade Inspection H.Q. B4 2nd Army at HAZEBROUCK.	OA

2449 Wt. W14957/Mgo 750,000 1/16 J.B.C. & A. Forms/C.2118/12.

WAR DIARY FOR MONTH OF APRIL, 1917.

VOLUME:- 14

UNIT:- A.D.V.S. 16th Division

Army Form C. 2118.

WAR DIARY
or
INTELLIGENCE SUMMARY

A.D.V.S
16th Div

(Erase heading not required.)

Instruct regarding War Diaries and Intelligence Summaries are contained in F.S. Regs., Part II. and the Staff Manual respectively. Title Pages will be prepared in manuscript.

Place	Date	Hour	Summary of Events and Information	Remarks and references to Appendices
LOCRE. M29.b.3.9. (FRANCE sheet 28.S.W.)	1.4.17	a.m.	Visit H.Q. 77 H.A.F.A. Bde. LA CLYTTE. Interview ADVS 19th Div. Also his men to an WESTOUTRE area	J.O.T.A.
	2.4.17	a.m.	2 LA CLYTTE. See O.C. 77th Bde. in reference to Disability cases. Visit all wounds of Infantry transport. See Capt. F. BROAD (V.O. of 77th Bde. R.F.A.) in horse for vaccination tomorrow to 47 MVS. — 19th Div. L MVS moved to new site yesterday	J.O.T.A.
	3.4.17	a.m.	Superintend internment of 40 animals at WITTENHOEK Siding. Delay — owing to hole dug hall of ground being too shallow, the floor of truck became very slippery & difficult, the floor of truck became not up slippery & difficult. Several stores to fill. Interview ADVS 47th Div.	J.O.T.A.
			With O.C. in fact all animals of 180th Bde. R.F.A. — 33 Disability cases selected for evacuation, but a few of these must be retained as spares, no Brigade made to to having area over 6 in want.	J.O.T.A.
	4.4.17	a.m.		
	5.4.17	a.m.	Visit c/ 77 Bde. + 47 MVS. Inspect transport of 49th Inf. Bde. Also horses of D.H.Q. + MP. Visit new site for MVS with O.C. 11th HANTS (P) in reference Battalion transport. Horses look in good condition directly been hardly to having Rebecca in the open in severe weather. Visit 47 MVS.	J.O.T.A.
	6.4.17	a.m.	Visit O.C. TRAIN at RENINGHELST. Conference of V.O.s at office. 47 MVS evacuate to 20 animals by days from BAC SAN MAUR	J.O.T.A.

2449 Wt. W14957/Mgo 750,000 1/16 J.B.C. & A. Forms/C.2118/12.

Army Form C. 2118.

WAR DIARY
or
INTELLIGENCE SUMMARY
(Erase heading not required.)

ADVS
16th Div.

Place	Date	Hour	Summary of Events and Information	Remarks and references to Appendices
LOCRE	7/4/17	am pm	Visit 48th Inf. Bde. 112th Fd Ambulance, Y/14 Coy A.S.C. and 2nd ARMY Training area Call at N&23 V&2 Hospital Form STOMATITIS cases recently evacuated from this Div. — Call to see D.D.V.S. at 2nd Army H.Q.	J.A.
	8/4/17	am	Inspect 158 & 152 Coys. R.E. Capt REID A.V.C. proceeds on leave	
			V&t 47 M.V.S.	J.A.
	9/4/17	am pm	Inspect 142, 143 & 144 Coys A.S.C. Inspected all transport (4) of Inf. Bde.	J.A.
			of res 47 M.V.S. evacuated 11 animals to vet stores to-nt	J.A.
	10/4/17	am	Inspect 157 Coy R.E. & 7%1/1 & 3 Sections D.A.C.	
		pm	Inspect 113th Fd Ambulance Officer	J.A.
	11/4/17	am	Inspect A 13 C. & D 1/177 Bde. — Inspect in condition	
			Sid cases at D.H.Q. Officers Wire ADVS 3rd Aust L. Bun — lost	
			for 8 places on battn on 13th	
	12/4/17	am	Visit 47 M.V.S. & invest failed by letter, re enemy prophetaxis	J.A.
		pm	Officer sick cases — S.H.Q.	
	13/4/17	am	Visit 113th A.F.A. Bde. advanced section arrived at house	
			yesterday, remainder arrive today. Visit 47 M.V.S.	
		pm	Conference of V.Os. officers ESTAIRES.	J.A.
	14/4/17	am	41 cars. by train	
			Inspect 113th N Bde. A.F.A. & also L 681 L.D. 48 H.D. for full evacuation — also select about 40 forward animal trans for S. L. City.	
		pm	Visit D.D.V.S. at 2nd Army H.Q.	J.A.

WAR DIARY
or
INTELLIGENCE SUMMARY

Army Form C. 2118.

A.D.V.S.
16th Division

Place	Date	Hour	Summary of Events and Information	Remarks and references to Appendices
LOCRE.	15.4.17	a.m.	Inspect D.R. Lt. cars of 11th Hants (P.) Inspect two ambulance waggons with H.Q.Q. & Q.M.g. section & fow 11th Hants transport at M23.a.7.4. Official copy of arrangement for collection of sick in the event of an advance sent to M.V.O. Interview O.C. 11th Hants transport of 11th Hants moves to M.23.a.	
	16.4.17	a.m.	O.C. 113 F.A. Ambulance, & send suggestions for improvement of details management.	
			47 M.V.S. vaccinate 52 animals by road to ST. OMER. Visit waggon lines of 113 H.F.A. Bde. & MANGE CAMPS. Visit M.V.S. & V.O. of AUST 3rd AUSTRALIAN Divn. to 12 Pl. Cairo and charge - train by road ADVS 3rd AUSTRALIAN	
	17.4.17	a.m.	Interview ADVS 36th Divn re ambulance - train by rail. Horse Pipe. Rifle also two sections (2 motor & 1 pair horse drawn) to 113 F.B.A.C. A.F.A. Bde.	
		p.m.	Inspect 11th Hants - R.A.M.C. cars & horse ambulance lined up & ambulance limpeck hospital arrangements of 48th Inf. Bde. - return from 2 ARMY training area.	
	18.4.17	a.m. p.m.	Visit 49th Inf Bde. & 180th Bde. R.F.A. in trenches. Draw chargers for O.C. 112 & C.112 of F.A. and from 23 V.F. Hospital ST. OMER on the way to D.D.R.2 Army.	
	19.4.17	a.m.	Reconnaissance of the two from D.H.Q. Baoks by trolley to H.O. B cranes work on new MVS site, Corpo water Backs objectay to it. The site has been surveyed by Royal Engineers, & 12 lads of road material laid down together with a trial gate lamps erected by Lieut ?? transport. Visit 112 F.A. Ambs & 11th Hants transport lines.	

War Diary or Intelligence Summary

Army Form C. 2118.

A.D.V.S.
16th Div.

Place	Date	Hour	Summary of Events and Information	Remarks and references to Appendices
LOC RE	24.4.17	am	Visit to Artery wagon lines of 180th Bde R.F.A. Inspect D/180. Selecting 10 horses for evacuation Dublin.	
		pm	Inspect Vet'y Hosp to horses & mules. Inspect C/180 Bde. Selected 14 DbLty cases for evacuation.	
	25.4.17	am	Visit 47 M.V.S. Telephone D.D.V.S. 2nd Army who photo an enquiry in re 3 inspected A/180 Bde. Available for evacuation 13 DbLty cases for evacuation.	
		pm	Visit D/180 Bde. Weapon line & inspect 10 M.V.S.	
	26.4.17	am	Inspect H.Q. horses, & D/180 Bde R.F.A. Visit 47 M.V.S.	
		pm	Inspect 142 Coy A.S.C.	
	27.4.17	am	Reconnoitre road BEECHE & STAPLE. Prepared convoy to evacuate 10 horses to ST OMER. Vents not fit sick HORSE HALTS.	
		pm	Conference of V.Os. Visit 47 M.V.S. Instructions being given by D.D.M.S. IX Corps at march of incinerator. Latrine etc. ordered to be completed before Section moves in.	
	28.4.17	am	47 M.V.S. evacuated 12 horses by convoy from BAC SAN MAUR	
		pm	Visit Sanitary Officer at new M.V.S. site, to decide position of incinerator. The Inspect B/113 Bde AFA. Some horse rough. W. Plate Insp. D.A.Q.M.G. Inspect A/Sho. Visit location of new ware hanging to 180th Bde R.F.A. of Sho. h.29. M.16.d. 1.8. Officer. Recommended from D.D.V.S. that not to Chelmunt. Horses of M.V.S. to be still further reduced by S-Ride.	
	29.4.17	am	office	
	30.4.17	am	20 47 M.V.S. Instruct forest't for evacuate M.V.S. evacuate 25 horses Inspect 110 Hat. G. Framitts. Visit 2nd Dublin Div. to STOMER B6.	
		pm	There are now no cases of MANGE in the Division.	

Army Form C. 2118.

WAR DIARY
or
INTELLIGENCE SUMMARY
(Erase heading not required.)

Instructions regarding War Diaries and Intelligence Summaries are contained in F.S. Regs., Part II. and the Staff Manual respectively. Title Pages will be prepared in manuscript.

A.D.V.S. 16th Division

Place	Date	Hour	Summary of Events and Information	Remarks and references to Appendices
LOCRE	6.5.17	a.m.	2nd Lt. H.D.A.Q.M.G. visit 112th Fd. to Ambulance - LA CLYTTE, sir. S.H.D. + I amb. killed by shell fire during night at A, - 10 other wounded. Arrange forward evacuation of wounded by motor ambulance to rearward. Visit 47 M.V.S.	
		p.m.	Office. Visit 47 M.V.S. + inspect animals for remounts by road.	
	7.5.17	a.m. p.m.	Visit No. 13 Veterinary Hospital - NEUFCHATEL. 4 billets owners examined. D.C. & D/17 Bde A.F.A. at no 157 Engr. Regt.	
	8.5.17	a.m.	Enfield B.C. & D/17 Bde. at No. 157 Engr. Regt.	
		p.m.	to ST. ANSCAPEL, in L. cav of M. DEREVAL for keep of sick & wounded. Inspect convoy of 4 J.M.V.S. 1 shell wounded arm ambulance. to STOMER by motor ambulance.	
	9.5.17	a.m.	Inspect 177th Bde A.F.A. - adv to the area.	
		p.m.	gn. ammunition in rear of ANTI-GAS HORSE RESPIRATOR at 47 M.V.S. Two animals (still wounded) sent over to motor ambulance to STOMER.	
	10.5.17	a.m.	Inspect transport of 47 & 46th Inf Bdn, occy M.G. Coy, visits ammunition lines at 11th Hants Regt.(?) & A/177 Bde R.F.A.	
		p.m.	Office. Visit 47 M.V.S. & inspect horses for warm bath.	
	11.5.17	a.m.	Visit 11th Han to. Transport Lines, & to B.M.V.S. sets at M.I.S. Cl. Inspect wagon lines of B.C. & D/180 Bde. turn to O.C. 180th Bde. & inspect owing entanglements. - wounded Royale.	
		p.m.	Conference of V. O. - officers M.V.S. & Veterinary	

JOHN MAUR

Army Form C. 2118.

WAR DIARY
or
INTELLIGENCE SUMMARY

(Erase heading not required.)

A.D.V.S.
16th Div.

(3)

Place	Date	Hour	Summary of Events and Information	Remarks and references to Appendices
LOCRE.	12.5.17	a.m.	2 horses evacuated from 47 M.V.S. by motor ambulance to STOMER. Inspect C/113th Bde. A.F.A. who have moved 2 new wagon lines today.	
		p.m.	Office. Skin eruption now common at B/110 Bde, chu. ACARUS SARCOPS. Visit H.Q. 180th Bde. R.F.A. & 47 M.V.S. See horse cases at B/180 Bde. Visit purchases & site of transport lines.	
	13.5.17	a.m.	Visit 47 M.V.S. & inspect holmes of evacuations from Suspect 142 Coy. A.S.C.	
		p.m.	Office.	
	14.5.17	a.m.	Funkers P.M. evacuation and forward D.H.Q. - Ruptie Brigham Office.	
		p.m.	Visit 47 & 2 mule two & 7/8 mule two transport lines. Also 47 M.V.S. 42 M.V.S. evacua_ to STOMER.	
	15.5.17	a.m.	Visit 180 Bde. wagon lines. 47 M.V.S. Lieut. CAWTHORN A.V.C. temporarily takes over command of 47 M.V.S. while Capt. LENTON is on leave.	
		p.m.	Visit transport lines of 2 mule two T.M. & 49th Bde. re transfer of certain charge animals.	
	16.5.17	a.m.	Visit D&C/113th Bde. A.F.A. & 47 M.V.S. CAPT. LENTON A.V.C. proceeds on leave. Inspect 112th & F.A. 7314th Road Construction Party. Visit lines of Traffic Control Party - 24 horses (Cav)	
	17.5.17	a.m.	Inspect horses of D.H.Q. & M.M.P. Visit 47 M.M.T. & HAEGEDOORNE. Ratched re forwards arrangement for evacuating horses before entraining.	
		p.m.	Inspect transport of 4th Co. B. transaued, recently arrived in this area. Several cases of Sarcoptie Mange in this unit, which have been ingeed with sulphur & sent to mobile hospital.	

J.O.A.

War Diary / Intelligence Summary

Army Form C. 2118

A.D.V.S. 16th Div.

Place	Date	Hour	Summary of Events and Information	Remarks and references to Appendices
LOC R.E.	18.5.17	am	Inspect with Capt. REID, A.V.C. transport of 4th COLDSTREAM GUARDS. Result – 30 SARCOPTIC MANGE, 11 Suspicious. SARCOPS at once. Suspicious Serapups from 2 cases shewed ACARUS SARCOPS. Give man leave, send to M.V.S. remainder cases to limp, all animals to be kept tomorrow. Inspect D/177 Bde. R.F.A. – visit 47 M.V.S.	
	19.5.17	pm	Conference of V.Os. office M.V.S. march of animals. Inspect 113th D.A.C., also Suspects – Skin + Debility cases of D/113 Bde. A.F.A. – Visit 47 M.V.S.	
		pm	Inspect C.O. motor all animals of 4 COLDSTREAM GUARDS, including 2 Cl. KEMMEL SHELTERS. Select 4 299 horses for O? MANGE camp for new cases.	
	20.5.17	am	Visit 47 M.V.S. Inspect horses for vaccination. Ordered water tank. Have arrived. Bought from there to have saddle, a metal bracket will take to the Armoury.	
	21.5.17	am	Visit wagon lines of 59th & 59th Bde. R.F.A. & 11 Bde. R.F.A. & H.D.A.C., also thin are bad night. Badly affected with lice, to large numbers. Afraid to have MANGE. Late phone A.D.V.S. 11th Div. & told him that horses are being summoned and to shew in own division. Visit H.Q. 36th Bn. + 72nd Section 16th D.A.C. Office. Reconnoiter new cross country tracks from KEMMEL to OC R.E.	
	22.5.17	am	Inspect B + C /77 Bde. R.F.A. – Visit 47 M.V.S.	
		pm	Office. Turn of 13 = 9 Remounts for Divisions at WITTENHOCK. A.D.V.S. 11 Div ... in rear of horse Depot.	

Army Form C. 2118.

WAR DIARY
or
INTELLIGENCE SUMMARY
(Erase heading not required.)

A.D.V.S.
16th Div.

Place	Date	Hour	Summary of Events and Information	Remarks and references to Appendices
LOC RE.	23.5.17	a.m.	Inspect & view 159 Remounts recvd for the Divnal. 107 of them were unfit for artillery. Visit 47 MVS (previous to admit. all men of MANGE cases of 4 Col Battery arriving there). Go to M.V.S. for Fin. Lunch. 5th Army R.H.A Bgr. arriving in this area. Capt HUNTER R.A.V.C. in vet'nary charge office. Visit 11th HANTS(P) + A(?) BSr amm. Col D.H.Q. + 5th Army R.H.A. BSr. (3rd Bn. Horse + Bn.C)	
	24.5.17	p.m.	Visit amm col D.H.Q. + 5th Army R.H.A Bgr. (3rd Bn Horse + Bn C) Visit 47 M.V.S.	
	25.5.17	p.m. a.m.	office. Inspect 113 of sick amb. Reported to 16th D.A. HQ that re causes of MANGE in Bgr. but as city afferent amongst animals. Visit 48th + 49th Inf Bgr. Transport lines, + unit DAPM & inspected one Transport & proposed removal to ave VIII wagons + transport lines.)	
	27.5.17	a.m. p.m.	Conference of V.O.S. Inspect 4 Cob't Field Bakery transport. Remounts had hasty EECKE + STAPLE to HQ 48 Sick Horse hats taking N.C.O. -/c construction party from M.V.S.	
	28.5.17	a.m. p.m.	Two mares rec'd are uneased by Slave by H.Q. Visit 5th Army R.H.A BSr + 47 M.V.S., Inspecting Horses in new location. Visit 47 M.V.S. with Lt Col Eden A.D.V.S 2nd Army to arrange for selected Sick in train in to trucks for Life & ? ambulance passage. Visit H.Q. 180th BSr. R.F.A. Inspect Horses + sale - stables must be put + 314 Rd Construction Co'y. Horses + Stf Control Establishment Mcki and Stable Row tide & dirty. Visit Inf Transport lines (Shelling & turns on my arrival.	
	29.5.17	a.m. p.m.	have inspected in animals convictions among animals. It present going on was very kind. Some taken. Visit Rmt off Horses + officers & mens kits 47 M.V.S. office. Sick horses passed in -20 animals sent H.Q.	

WAR DIARY
or
INTELLIGENCE SUMMARY

(6)

Army Form C. 2118.

A.D.V.S.
16th Div.

Place	Date	Hour	Summary of Events and Information	Remarks and references to Appendices
LOC.R.E.	30.5.17	am	Visit 180th Bde. R.F.A. wagon lines, inspected horses of 9/1/180 Bde. Visit 47 M.V.S. – 2 animals evacuated by motor ambulance.	
		pm	Office. Thus' A.D.V.S. 11th Division at 47 M.V.S. Two paddocks for Debility cases opened at M.V.S.	
	31.5.17	am	Inspected D.H.Q. horses, 8 animals on "Debility" paddock. Capt. KENTON A.V.C. returned from leave.	
		pm	Office. Inspected M.M.P. & Traffic Control Detachment horses at terminal A.D.V.S. 1st Division.	

MANGE. – Practically all cases which have come into the Division, have been sent by us to the Division, and further outbreak MANGE.

SHELL FIRE – 5 through Area VIII – (Our transport have on his way) have checked up fighting & important work, and all our animals have always remained. 5 horses were wounded to reports, before being commenced, obtained but hay. Horses received full rations as well as grazing, & in a few days shown great improvement.

J. Anderson
Major
A.D.V.S. 16th Div.

WAR DIARY.

FOR MONTH OF JUNE, 1917.

VOLUME:- 19

UNIT:- DADVS. 16th Division

WAR DIARY or INTELLIGENCE SUMMARY

Army Form C. 2118.

A.D.V.S.
16th Div.

Place	Date	Hour	Summary of Events and Information	Remarks and references to Appendices
LOCRE	1.6.17	a.m.	Inspected 48th Inf Bde Transport. Visited 47th & 49th Inf Bde Transport Lines.	
		p.m.	Conference of V.O.s. Visited 47 M.V.S. Inspected debility camp in Baggage Pk.	
	2.6.17	a.m.	Inspected 11 hauls transport, & horses of 180th Bde. Advanced depôt two. Sick horses in debility passed back to be returned to units. Saw O.C. 728 French Tramway Cy. Re returns. Visited 47 M.V.S. Reported re-covering of SPIROCHAETE in blood serum of JAUNDICE case 15 D.D.R.S.	
	3.6.17	a.m.	Debility cases, unopened & in doubt, returned to their units as had lack in remaining as a camping ground. Visited Div ↑	
			Bde H.Q.s. 2nd Army Hd-qrs etc.	
	4.6.17	a.m.	Visited 47 M.V.S. Inspected cars for warm free	
			M.V.S. warmth 2 animals by motor ambulance Cars & 6 by road to ST OMER. Inspected 49th Inf Bde Transport.	
			2 horses of 1st Div Amm. Sub & 2 of Div Two Res returned	
			Cols. Visited 47 M.V.S.	
		p.m.	Inspected Animals in advanced supply columns of 2nd Army R.H.A. Bde - unopened.	
	5.6.17	a.m.	Office. Ordered temp ADV. D.H.Q. - interview Q.O.C. 16th Division	
		p.m.	Visit 47 M.V.S. 2 horses by motor ambulance to OMER. 2 horses by motor ambulance to OMER.	
	6.6.17	10am	L.O.C.R.E. visit to Field Animal casualty officer. Inspect 13. C.D./ 180.Bd. R.F.a;- see JAUNDICE case Vept A/180 Bde & 47 R.H.A.	
			hers of cases Evacuation by from 47 M.V.S. Transport with J. B. Ste &

Army Form C. 2118.

WAR DIARY
or
INTELLIGENCE SUMMARY
(Erase heading not required.)

4 D.V.S.
16th Div.

(2)

Place	Date	Hour	Summary of Events and Information	Remarks and references to Appendices
LOCRE	7.6.17	a.m.	Visit H.Q. Board at MONT ROUGE, & inspected D.H.Q. Horses. Visit 47 M.V.S.	
		p.m.	Office. Artillery wagon lines advanced to N.E. of KEMMEL. Spent aft. N.16 & 21.- also 1.28. Amm. trains Horse lines have advanced to beyond WYTSCHAETE ridge.	
	8.6.17	a.m.	Visit wagon lines of 177 Bde. R.F.A. 180 Bde. R.F.A. 113 Bde. R.F.A. & 16 D.A.C.	
		p.m.	Visit KEMMEL to select site for Advanced Detachment of 47 M.V.S. Lieut. CAWTHORN A.V.C. transferred to 47 M.V.S. to take command of Detachment. Conference of V.Os.	
	9.6.17	a.m.	Inspected 47th Dvl. B.Sn. Transport, & Visit 47 M.V.S.	
		p.m.	Visit Advanced Collecting Station at N.21.C.26 (sheet 28). Detachment from 47 M.V.S.- (1 N.C.O. & 2 men A.V.C. - 1 ASC driver with Horse ambulance), & Lieut. CAWTHORN in command, moved up this morning.	
	10.6.17	p.m.	47 M.V.S. evacuated 30 animals to IX Corps Veterinary Detachment at Railhead.	
		p.m.	20 47 M.V.S. selected cases for reserve.	
	11.6.17	a.m.	Visit 1.180 Bde. wagon lines, & Advanced Visit & Detachment at N.21.C.26. Detachment returns to Section today. Wagon lines have returned to rear area. Our guns & A.T.C. still up their new charge at D. & DI by day - heavy shelling.	
		p.m.	Inspect Remounts of 11th Hants. (D.) Coy, reinf 47 M.V.S.	
	12.6.17	a.m.	Remounts Horse Drivers up to move to MERRIS area. Tournay, Eng. Artillery, R.T.N, Reserve. Visit 47 M.V.S. also Advanced Detachment, & 180 & 113 Bde. R.F.A. at N.21.E. assisting of horses & find arrangements satisfactory.	J.A.J.

Army Form C. 2118.

WAR DIARY
or
INTELLIGENCE SUMMARY

(Erase heading not required.)

A.D.V.S.
16th Div

Place	Date	Hour	Summary of Events and Information	Remarks and references to Appendices
LOCRE.	13.6.17	10am	Travs. with Hd. Qrs. the Division, call at M.V.S.	
		3pm	47 M.V.S. went to draw M26 b.8.8. (sheet 27) after ne came up. 33 animals to IX Corps Vet. Detachment.	
MERRIS	"	11.30am	arrive	
	14.6.17	7pm	47 M.V.S. arrive & go into Camp at F7.b.6.3. (sheet 36A)	
		8am	Interview D.D.V.S. at 2nd Echelon Hd. Qrs. 2nd ARMY re remount transport area	
			office	
	15.6.17	9am	Visit Hd. Qrs. & all units of 47th Inf. Bde. & look into arrangements supply for animals. Inspect B.H.Q. horse	
		2pm	office. Visit 47 M.V.S.	
	16.6.17	9am	Visit 149th M.G. Coy. Hd. Qrs. 49th Bde. Transport lines - 47th & 8th Dennis Str.	
		2pm	office - 47 M.V.S. issue to 12 animals to IX Corps M.V. Detachment	
	17.6.17	11am	Return again to many floods over roads in LOCRE area	
			wrote H.Q. the Div. re Everton for LOCRE area	
LOCRE.	"	9am	47 M.V.S. leave F7.b.6.3. (sheet 36A)	
		12 noon	arrive, after visiting 4 M.V.S. at M26 b.8.8.	
	18.6.17	1am	Received orders to return to MERRIS. area	
		10am	visit D.A.D.M.G. warning & arrange 88 Remounts to which have arrived by rail from CALAIS - for over-charge	
MERRIS.		1pm	Interview A.D.V.S. 111 Div. re 4.9.05 temp. to Lt. for his area. Capt. LENTON adm. Hd. Qr. 111 F.A. - Lieut. CAWTHORN taken over M.V.S. 4) M.V.S. at M26 b.8.8.	
		7pm	arrive. Office. Visit & inspect sick at 144 & 145 Coys A.S.C. & Spare Epp. R.S.C.	

War Diary

A.D.V.S.
16th Div.

Place	Date	Hour	Summary of Events and Information	Remarks
MERRIS	19.6.17	a.m.	By car, visit 142 Coy. A.S.C. + obt. sick of 47 M.V.S. at M 26.b.8.8. Sick & Evac. Left there + had conversation & re-natures to S.O. - ordered etc - taken - PA. MINCHINTON, to inform to 47 M.V.S. Office. - The following personnel on detachment with IX Corps. - 1 N.C.O. + 3 Pts from IX Corps. M.V.S. battn at I.D.R. station IX Corps Horse Dep.	
"	20.6.17	8.30 a.m.	Leave with D.H.Q.	
GODEVER-SVELDE	"	9 a.m.	Arrive. By car V. to STOMER to attend Conference at 23 M.V.2 Hospital. D.V.S. D.Ds.V.S. + A.Ds.V.S.	
"	21.6.17	a.m.	Visit 48th & D.H.Q. + various emb. & transport lines in 48th Bn.	
	"	p.m.	Visit 47 M.V.S. - Officer. M.V.S. ev at E.3. arr. Co. to M.V. Detachment at BOESCHEPE. Capt L. LENTON reports from to Leave with D.H.Q.	
ZEGGERS-CAPPEL	22.6.17	8.30 a.m.	Arrive. Arrange for 47 M.V.S. to billet S. of Farm	
	"	10 a.m.	with. Capt L. LENTON running command of Section. Lieut. CAWTHORN returning to H.Q. 2nd Train	
	"	3 p.m.	47 M.V.S. arrives from Q.6.Y.) (sheet 22) Capt LENTON finds new camp for M.V.S. at B.19.d.7.6 + to move Section there to-morrow	
"	23.6.17	a.m.	V to VIII Corps. H.Q. + report B.A.D. v.s. at ESQUELBECQ. - 347 M.V.S. move to B.19.d.7.6	
		p.m.	Visit 47 M.V.S.	

JOA

WAR DIARY.

FOR MONTH OF JULY, 1917.

VOLUME :- 20

UNIT :- D.A.D.V.S. 16 Division

Army Form C. 2118.

WAR DIARY
or
INTELLIGENCE SUMMARY

(Erase heading not required.)

D.A.D.V.S.
16 th Divn

Place	Date	Hour	Summary of Events and Information	Remarks and references to Appendices
ZEGGERS -CAPPEL	1/7/16	am	MAJOR ANDREWS hands over Enquhany to CAPT. LENTON, who will take over pending arrival of CAPT. DEVINE. A.D.V.S. proceeds NEUFCHATEL. MAJOR ANDREWS arrived to take over duties as D.A.D.V.S. and	
"		pm	MAJOR DEVINE arrived to take over duties as D.D.V.S. fifth Army took over from Capt LENTON. — DDVS notified by wire of MAJOR DEVINE's arrival. Received instructions from ADOS "K"Div. that no R. of Mr 137 KO RE was expected to the horse. Inspected all the riders and transport at 167 Div Headquarters. — Inspected Military Police Horses. —	
	3/7/16		Inspected 16th Divl Headquarters Signal Co Horses.	

Army Form C. 2118.

WAR DIARY
or
INTELLIGENCE SUMMARY

(Erase heading not required.)

D.A.D.V.S. 16th DIV (2)

Place	Date	Hour	Summary of Events and Information	Remarks and references to Appendices
ZEGGERS CAPPEL	4/7/17	A.M.	Inspected the horses at 49th Infy Bde Headqrs. 140 C.A.S.C. 2/Royal Irish R. and 49th M.G. Gun Co.	
"		P.M.	Inspected the horses of the 7th & 8th Royal Innis Fusiliers 4/6 Royal Irish Fusiliers	
"	5-7-17	A.M.	Inspected the horses of the 7th Royal Irish Rifles 7th 8th 9th & 10th Royal Dublin Fusiliers - all the Royal Irish Res. were found in a poor condition	
"	"		Inspected the 7th & 8th Machine Gun Co. and 148th Co. R.E.	
"	"	P.M.	Inspected the horses of the 6th Royal Irish Regt.	
			Inspected 4 7th Motd Veterinary Section, and the horses for inoculation	

WAR DIARY or INTELLIGENCE SUMMARY

Army Form C. 2118.

Place	Date	Hour	Summary of Events and Information	Remarks and references to Appendices
Zaggers Cappel	9/7/19	Am	Inspected #7 Mobile Vety Section and the horses of the 112th Field Ambulance.	
		Pm	Inspected the horses of 6th Royal Irish Regiment. Capt LUCKING V.O. i/c 177th Bde R.F.A. instructed to take Vety charge of 180th Bde R.F.A. in addition to his Vety duties. Inspected the horses of the 1st Royal Munster Fus: and of the 111th Field Ambulance.	
	10/7/19	Am	Received wire from the adjutant 160th Bde R.F.A. reporting Capt ARMSTRONG's departure on the 9th to XIX Corps H.A. — Sent copy of wire to A.D.V.S. XIX Corps. Inspected #9 Mobile Vety Section.	

Army Form C. 2118.

WAR DIARY
or
INTELLIGENCE SUMMARY
(Erase heading not required.)

(5)

Instructions regarding War Diaries and Intelligence Summaries are contained in F. S. Regs., Part II. and the Staff Manual respectively. Title Pages will be prepared in manuscript.

Place	Date	Hour	Summary of Events and Information	Remarks and references to Appendices
JAGGERS CAPPEL	10-7-17	pm	Inspected 112th Field Ambulance horses.	
"	11-7-17	am	Inspected the horses of 47th Inf. Bde Hdqrs. 6th Con. Rangers 7th Leinsters & 6th Royal Irish and Inspected the horses B 4.7th Machine Gun Co. and of 143rd Co A.S.C.	
"		pm		
"	12-7-17		Inspected the horses of 2nd Royal Irish Rgt. 7th & 8th R. Innis. Fus. 7/8 R Irish Fus. 49th Mac Gun Co. and 113th Field Ambulance.	
	13/7/17		Inspected the horses from the 7th Leint. Rfls 7th, 8th & 9th Dublin Fusiliers. 48th Mac Gun Co 145th Co A.S.C.	

2449. Wt. W14957/Mgo 750,000 1/16 J.B.C. & A. Forms/C.2118/12.

Army Form C. 2118.

WAR DIARY
or
INTELLIGENCE SUMMARY

(6)

(Erase heading not required.)

Place	Date	Hour	Summary of Events and Information	Remarks and references to Appendices
JNNGERS CAPPEL	14/7/17		Inspected the horses of 156th & 157th Coy R.E. 11th Hants (Pioneers) and Headquarters B 11th Srd Bgn.	
~	15/7/17		Inspected the horses of 16th R.D. et Heavy mortars	
~	16/7/17		Inspected 16th Div Heavy Trench C. Inspected 47th M.Mort. Bty Aelyn	
~	17th am		Inspected the horses of 6th R Irish Regt. 6th Conn. Rangers. 7th Leinster Regt. 1st Royal Munster Fusrs & 145th Coy A.S.C.	
~	18th pm		Inspected the horses of 7th Royal Irish Rifles and 2nd Royal Dublin Fusrs.	
~			Inspected the 47th M.Mort. Vety Section	

WAR DIARY
or
INTELLIGENCE SUMMARY

Army Form C. 2118.

Place	Date	Hour	Summary of Events and Information	Remarks and references to Appendices
JAGGERS CAPPEL	23/7/17		The 47th M.V.S. moved to WINNEZEELE. Inspection of the 4 M.Gun Co. and 7th Royal Irish Rifles	
Poperinghe	24/7/17		16th Div Head Quarters moved from Jaggers Cappel to Poperinghe. Inspected the 47th Mobile Vety Section and the horses of 6th Royal Irish Regiment.	
"	25/7/17		Inspected the 16th D.A.C. — Sent instructions to O.C. 47th M.V.S. to move the section to WATOU on 26th.	
	26/7/17		Inspected the horses of 11th Hants and 47th Machine Gun Co.	
	27/7/17		Inspected Major 16 Div horses and Hops Signal Co horses.	

WAR DIARY or INTELLIGENCE SUMMARY

Army Form C. 2118.

(Erase heading not required.)

Place	Date	Hour	Summary of Events and Information	Remarks and references to Appendices
Poperinghe	28/7/17		Inspected 47th Mobile Vety Section. The horses of 1st Mountain Bty Amb Regt. 8th Lancs Fus. and 113th Field ambulance.	
			Attended conference at A.D.V.S. Office XIX Corps.	
		am	Inspected horses at 47th Bde (Infy) Headquarters.	
		pm	— 48th Bde (Infy) Headquarters.	
	29/7/17	am	Inspected the horses of 142 Co — 16th Div Train.	
		pm	Inspected the 47th M.V.S and all the A.V.C. Sgt drivers attached to the 16th Divn.	
	30/7/17		Inspected the horses 143, 144, 145th Co's 16th Div Train.	
			During the month air horses died or from medical treat and were disposed of —	
			5 from gunshot wounds. Two were destroyed — 8 for gunshot wounds and his for fractures — 8 for general conditions. 2 S.W horses being gunshot wounds. 11 for 72 horses were evacuated — 25 being gunshot wounds. 11 accidental gun poisoning. 8 mange. 4 cellulitis & arthritis. 11 exudative shivers. 8 chronic lameness. 1 tumour.	
			Brennan Dillon major. A.D.V.S. 16th Division.	

WAR DIARY.

FOR MONTH OF AUGUST, 1917.

VOLUME 2

UNIT D.A.D.V.S. 16 Division

WAR DIARY or INTELLIGENCE SUMMARY

Army Form C. 2118.

DADVS 16th Division

Place	Date	Hour	Summary of Events and Information	Remarks and references to Appendices
Poperinghe	1/8/17	12 noon	Attended conference at ADVS. Office XIX Corps.	
"	2/8/17	am	Inspected the horses of 76th Field Amb. R.A. & harnesses	
			Inspected the horses at 16th Divl Headquarters -	
			Inspected the 47th Mobile Vety Section and harnesses	
		pm	Held conference of Officers with the V.Os. of the Division	
"	3/8/17	am	Inspected the horses at 47th Mobile Vety. Section for evacuation	
			Inspected the horses of Headquarters Co. 16th Divl Train. and 46th Coy 13th Headquarters. DADVS gave lectures & demonstrations of the application of and after three Respirators at H.Qro. Co. 16th Divl Train.	
Brandhoek Camp.	4/8/17 am		The 16th Divl Headquarters moved from Poperinghe to Brandhoek Camp 2 mls East of Vlamertinghe. Attended conference at ADVS. Office XIV Corps.	
	5/8/17 pm		Inspected the horses of 145th Co. A.S.C.	
	6/8/17		Inspected the horses of 7th Irish Rifles. 2nd, 8th & 9th Royal Dublin Fusiliers and 4 8th Machine gun Co.	

WAR DIARY or INTELLIGENCE SUMMARY

Army Form C. 2118.

Place	Date	Hour	Summary of Events and Information	Remarks and references to Appendices
BRANDHOEK CAMP.	6/8/17	am	Inspected the 16th D.A.C. Inspected the horse buoyards of 47th Machine Gun Co, 6th Conn Rangers, 1st Munsters	
		pm	Inspected the Company with the O.C. 16th Div. Train. The horse of 142, 143, 144, 145 Coys R.A.C. 16th Div. Train.	
"	7/8/17	am	Inspected 180th Bde R.F.A. and the transport lines of 49th Machine Gun Co.	
"		pm	Inspected the horses of 7th & 6th Royal Innis. Fus. 2nd Royal Irish Regt. and the 76th Royal Irish Fus.	
	8/8/17	am	Inspected 180th Bde in company with A.D.V.S. XIX Corps 180th Bde R.F.A. and 49th Infy Bde.	
"		pm	Inspected the horses 16th Div. Signal Co. Examined the skin scrapings taken from five horses of D Batty 180th Bde R.F.A.	
"	9/8/17	am	Interviewed D.D.R. fifth army. 11 horses of 16th Div. Train which had been returned as H.D. were reclassified as L.D. and 5 mules reclassified to 180 Bde R.F.A. as L.D were reclassified to Pack by D.D.R.	

WAR DIARY
INTELLIGENCE SUMMARY

Army Form C. 2118.

(3)

Place	Date	Hour	Summary of Events and Information	Remarks and references to Appendices
BRAND HOEK CAMP.	9/6/17	p.m.	Inspected Advanced Posts of Mobile Vety Section at Hr 17 C.4.5. Scherp. 28. (known Belgium)	
"	10/6/17	a.m.	Inspected the horses for evacuation at 47th Mob. Vet. Sec.	
			Inspected the horses of 155th, 156th & 157th Field Coys RE	
		p.m.	Held Conference of Vety. Os. at Ypres.	
			Capt Lucking A.V.C. V.O. to 177th Bde RFA returned from leave in England.	
"	11/6/17	a.m.	Inspected MMP horses - Inspected the horses at 47 MVS for evacuation.	
		p.m.	Attended Conference at ADVS office XIX Corps.	
"	12/6/17	a.m.	Inspected the horses of 11th Hussars in Reserve.	
"	13/6/17	a.m.	Inspected 100 horses for Evacuation at 47th Mobile Vety Sec.	
		p.m.	Inspected Advanced Post of Mobile Vety Section.	
"	14/6/17	a.m.	Attended Wippenhoek Rail head and inspected the horses of Men.	
			from which have being evacuated.	

WAR DIARY / INTELLIGENCE SUMMARY

Army Form C. 2118.

Place	Date	Hour	Summary of Events and Information	Remarks and references to Appendices
BRANDHOEK CAMP	14/8/17	—	Inspected 43 horses received from 5th Australian Divn for Spare horse C.	
"	"	pm	D.A.D.V.S. gave lecture on horse management to offrs & Spare C.	
"	15/8/17	am	Inspected the horses of 177th Bde R.F.A	
"	"	pm	Inspected the horses of 11th Hants (Pioneers)	
"	16/8/17	am	Inspected the horses at 16 Mobile Vety Hosp & the horses of the Hops Transpt Co	
"	17/8/17	pm	Conference of M.O's at Divn'l office	
"	"	am	Inspected the horses for Spare horse at 47 M.V.S.	
"	"	pm	Inspected the horse trans at 16 M.V.S.A.C	
WATOU	18/8/17		The 16th Division moved to WATOU area	
"	19/8/17		Inspected 47th Mob. Vet Sec.	
"	20/8/17		Inspected 47th Infantry Bde.	
"	21/8/17		D.A.D.V.S. proceeded on leave to U.K.	
"	"		The 16th Divn Hqrs & Sup/y Bde moved to Achiet le Pet	
ACHIET le PETIT	27/8/17		D/Asst Caretkr S.H. 53304 reported for duty to D/177th Bde R.F.A	
"	28/8/17		The 16 Divn Hqrs moved to Moyenneville	

WAR DIARY.

FOR MONTH OF AUGUST, 1917.

VOLUME 22

UNIT A.D.V.S. 16th Division.

Vol 22

Army Form C. 2118.

A. & Q.
2 OCT 1917

WAR DIARY L.D.A.D.V.S.
or
INTELLIGENCE SUMMARY. 16th Division

(Erase heading not required.)

Instructions regarding War Diaries and Intelligence Summaries are contained in F. S. Regs., Part II. and the Staff Manual respectively. Title pages will be prepared in manuscript.

Month .... 16th DIVISION

Place	Date	Hour	Summary of Events and Information	Remarks and references to Appendices
Moyenneville	1/9/17	am	Attended Conference at Office of ADVS. VI Corps HQrs.	
		pm	Routine	
	2/9/17		Inspected 47th Mobile Vety Section and their arrangements for Evacuation at Boiry Ste Rictrude.	
	3/9/17	am	Inspected the horses of 180th Bde R.F.A.	
		pm	Inspected the horses of 177th Bde R.F.A.	
	4/9/17	am	Inspected the horses of 16th Divl Train.	
		pm	Inspected the horses of 16th Dublins, 2nd Royal Irish, 157th Field Co R.E. and 11th Hants.	
	5/9/17	am	Inspected the horses of 6th Royal Irish Reg, 6th Connaught Rangers, 7/8th Inniskillings, 1st Munsters.	
		pm	Inspected the horses of 4/7th Machine Gun Co, 48th Mac Gun Co, 8/9th Royal Irish Riffs, 11/13th R.I. Rif.	
	6/9/17	am	Inspected the animals of 16th Bn. M.G.C., 111th & 112th Field Ambulances.	
		pm	Conference of NCOs of the Divn at Offices of D.A.D.V.S.	

WAR DIARY or INTELLIGENCE SUMMARY

Army Form C. 2118.

(2)

Place	Date	Hour	Summary of Events and Information	Remarks and references to Appendices
MOYENNEVILLE	7/9/17	am	Inspected the horses of 180th Bde & 177 Bde R.F.A. and 16th D.A.C. with Havresacks VI Corps.	
		pm	Inspected the horse of 47th 48th & 49th Infantry Bdes with Havresacks VI Corps.	
	8/9/17	a.m	Attended conference at Offres. A.D.V.S. VI Corps.	
	9/9/17	a.m	Inspected the horses at 16th Divl H.Q. & Signal Co.	
		p.m	Inspected the horses of 49th Bde (Infty) Headquarters	
		p.m	Inspected the horses preparatory to 47th Infy Bde. Co. company with the Veterinarian VI Corps inspected	
	10/9/17	am	The L.D. & Riding horses of 16 Divl. Train	
		pm	Inspected the horses of "A" Bat. 177 Bde R.F.A.	
	11/9/17	a.m	Inspected the horses and mules of 156th Co. R.E. at St LEDGER.	
		p.m	Inspected the 47th M. V.S.	
	12/9/17	am	Inspected the horses and mules of 155 Co. R.E. at Boiry Becquerelle and 49th Mac. Gun Co. at MOYENNEVILLE and 8th Royal Dublin Fus. at HAMLINCOURT	

WAR DIARY
INTELLIGENCE SUMMARY

Army Form C. 2118.

Place	Date	Hour	Summary of Events and Information	Remarks and references to Appendices
Moyenneville	13/9/17	am	Inspected the horses at 16th Div Headquarters & the horses of 16th Div Signal Co	
		pm	Conference of MO's at office ADVS	
	14/9/17	am	Inspected the horses at 177th Bde RFA Headquarters. Examined three sick serchings for mange from horses of 177th Bde R.F.A. negative result.	
	15/9/17	am	ADVS attended conference at office ADMS VI Corps.	
	16/9/17	am	Inspected the horses for evacuation at 47th MVS. Let see Couture.	
	17/9/17	am	Inspected the horses of 2nd Royal Irish Regt & 8th Yorkshires	
		pm	Inspected the horses of Royal Irish Fus. Capt Reid. AVC VO i/c 49th Inf Bde left for ten days leave in U.K.	
	18/9/17	am	Inspected the horses of 180th Bde R.F.A.	
		pm	Inspected 4 7th Mobile Vety Section. Inspected the horses of 145th Coy AVC	

WAR DIARY
INTELLIGENCE SUMMARY

Army Form C. 2118.

(5)

Place	Date	Hour	Summary of Events and Information	Remarks and references to Appendices
BEHAGNIES	26/9/17	a.m.	Inspected the transport lines of 2nd & 9th Dublins	
"	"	p.m.	Inspected the horses of 111th & 112th Field Ambulances.	
"	27/9/17	a.m.	Inspected the horses and mules of 8th & 10th Dublins	
"	"	"	Inspected the horses and mules of 156th & 157th Coy R.E.	
"	28/9/17	p.m.	Inspected the horses & mules of 156th Coy R.E. & 49th Infy Bde HqRs	
"	"	p.m.	Conference of Vety. Officers and officer i/c D.A.D.S. at 16th Divn HqRs – 16th Signal Co.	
"	29/9/17	a.m.	Inspected the horses and mules at 16 Div HqRs – 16th Signal Co.	
"	"	p.m.	London.	
"	30/9/17	a.m.	Inspected the horses and mules of 49th Infy Bde HqRs.	

Bernard de Sims. Major
A.V.C
30/9/17

Veterinary
16th Division

WAR DIARY

FOR MONTH OF OCTOBER, 1917.

UNIT A.D.V.S. 16 Division

VOLUME NUMBER 23

WAR DIARY by DADYS
or
INTELLIGENCE SUMMARY. 16th Division

Army Form C. 2118.

Place	Date	Hour	Summary of Events and Information	Remarks and references to Appendices
DeBAGNIES	1/10/17	am	Inspected the lines and works of 113th Field Ambulance at La Cauchie. Anton.	
	2/10/17	am	Inspected the Lines for Evacuation at 49th Mobile Vety Section	
		pm	Inspected the lines and works at the following units. Headquarters 48th Infy Bde. - 49th Machine Gun Co. - 2nd Royal Irish Regt.	
	3/10/17	am	Inspected the lines and works of C + D batteries 180th Bde RFA.	
		pm	Inspected the lines and works 1/1 Hants	
	4/10/17	am	In company with ADVS VI Corps inspected 47th Mobile Veterinary Section, 7/6 Royal Irish Fusiliers, 157th Co R.E., 10th Dublins, 2nd Royal Irish Regt. 8th Dublins and 48th Infy Bde Headquarters wagon lines	
	5/10/17	am	Inspected the lines and works of A + D Batteries 180th Bde R.F.A.	
		pm	Inspected A + B Batteries 177th Bde R.F.A	

Army Form C. 2118.

WAR DIARY
or
INTELLIGENCE SUMMARY.
(Erase heading not required.)

(3)

Instructions regarding War Diaries and Intelligence Summaries are contained in F. S. Regs., Part II. and the Staff Manual respectively. Title pages will be prepared in manuscript.

Place	Date	Hour	Summary of Events and Information	Remarks and references to Appendices
BEHAGNIES	14/10/17		Inspected the transport lines of 47th Inf Bde Headquarters and 48th Machine Gun Co.	
"	15/10/17	am	Inspected the horses & mules of 11th Hants. and A + B Batteries 177th Bde R.F.A.	
		pm	Inspected the horses & mules of 2nd & 9th Dublins	
"	16/10/17	am	Inspected the transport of South Irish Horse Regt of R.I.R. which joined the 16th Div on 15/10/17.	
		pm	Inspected the horses & mules of 7th Inniskillins, 6th Connaught 1st R.I.R. Munsters and 47th Machine Gun Co.	
"	17/10/17	am	Accompanied by Major General Edwards American Army inspected No 1 Section 16th D.A.C. and 16 Div'l Train	
"		pm	Inspected No 2 + 3 Sections of 16 D.A.C.	
"	18/10/17	am	Inspected the horses at 49 Bty B Bde Headquarters	
		pm	Inspected the horses & mules of 1st Munsters, 6 Connaughts and 7th Leinsters	
"	19/10/17	am	Inspected 47th Mobile Vety Section	
		pm	Conference of V.Os at Office of DADVS	

A 6915. Wt. W14422/M1160. 350,000 10/16. D. D. & L. Forms/C./2118/14.

WAR DIARY
or
INTELLIGENCE SUMMARY

Army Form C. 2118.

(4)

(Erase heading not required.)

Instructions regarding War Diaries and Intelligence Summaries are contained in F. S. Regs., Part. II. and the Staff Manual respectively. Title pages will be prepared in manuscript.

Place	Date	Hour	Summary of Events and Information	Remarks and references to Appendices
BEHAGNIES	20/10/17	am	Attended Conference of ADMS XVII Corps.	
"	21/10/17	am	Inspected the horse and mules of 1st Dublins which arrived on 20th 10 pm 16th Div.	
"	22/10/17	am	Inspected the transport of 49th Machine Gun Co. and 11th Hants.	
"	"	pm	Examined measurements of 2nd Company Inniskilling Dragoons. Cases in 160th Bde R.F.A.	
—	23/10/17	am	Inspected horses for evacuation at 47th Mobile Vety Section.	
—	24/10/17	am	Inspected No. 2 & 3 Sections 16th D.A.C.	
—	"	pm	Inspected 143rd Coy 16th Divl. Train	
—	25/10/17	pm	Inspected 11th Dublins 2nd R.I. Regt.	
—	"	pm	Inspected 15/7th Co. R.E.	
—	26/10/17	am	Inspected 47th Mobile Vety Section	
"	"	pm	Conference of A.D.Cs. with Col. Officer of D.A.D.V.S.	
"	27/10/17	pm	Attended Conference of ADVS VI Corps.	
"	29/10/17	am	Inspected lines at Divl. Headquarters & H.Qrs Signal Co.	
"	"	pm	Inspected 47th Mobile Vety Section	

Army Form C. 2118.

WAR DIARY
or
INTELLIGENCE SUMMARY.
(Erase heading not required.)

Instructions regarding War Diaries and Intelligence Summaries are contained in F.S. Regs., Part II. and the Staff Manual respectively. Title pages will be prepared in manuscript.

Place	Date	Hour	Summary of Events and Information	Remarks and references to Appendices
Behagnies	29/9/17	a.m	My Company with D.A.D.V.S. 16th Divin inspected the transport lines of 4th, 7th & 8th Machine Gun Co. 1st Royal Munster Fus. 2nd & 8/9th Dubliners & 7/8 R. Innis. Fus. & S.I.H. Examined damaged horse at A. Chief - to brand without and have euthanised - had 90 rocks were sent to have in some feet.	
"	30/9/17		Inspected H.J. Mobile Vety. Section.	
"	3/9/17	am	My company with D.A.D.V.S. 16th Divn. inspected the transport of 46th H.M.g. Bde. Hdqrs - 10th Dublins, 6th Royal Irish Regt - 1st Dublins. Inspected 48 animals of the 8th Dublins which are being released to remount Third army	

Brian De Burn Major
D.A.D.V.S. 16th Divn

WAR DIARY

FOR MONTH OF NOVEMBER, 1917.

VOLUME :- 24

UNIT :- A.D.V.S. 16 Division

Army Form C. 2118.

WAR DIARY By DADVS
or
INTELLIGENCE SUMMARY. 16th Division
(Erase heading not required.)

Place	Date	Hour	Summary of Events and Information	Remarks and references to Appendices
Béhagnies	1/4/17	a.m	Inspected the horses for evacuation at 47th Mobile Vety Section	
"	"	p.m	Inspected 156 & 157 Fd Coy R.E.	
"	2/4/17	a.m	Inspected no 3 Section 16th DAC	
"	"	p.m	Conference of VOs at Offices of DADVS	
"	3/4/17	a.m	Attended conference at Offices DDVS VI Corps Headquarters	
"	4/4/17	a.m	Inspected the transport horses 49th Infantry Bde Headquarters	
"	5/4/17	a.m	Inspected 177 Bde RFA	
"	"	p.m	Examined microscopically many scrapings taken from horses	
"	"	"	& 173 Bde RFA all negative	
"	6/4/17	a.m	In company with DADVMS inspected the transport of 47th Infy Bde	
"	"	p.m	Headquarters. Inspected the transport of 11th Hants	
"	"	"	and C & D Batteries B.160. 173 Bde R.F.A.	
"	7/4/17	a.m	Inspected no 3 section DAC	
"	"	p.m	Inspected Advanced Post of 47 MVS at St LEDGER	
"	8/4/17	a.m	Inspected Horse Supply & horses	
"	"	p.m	Conference of VOs at Office of DADVS	

WAR DIARY
INTELLIGENCE SUMMARY

Army Form C. 2118.

(3)

Place	Date	Hour	Summary of Events and Information	Remarks and references to Appendices
Béhagnies	18/11/17	a.m	Inspected Div: Transport of 1st R. Munsters & 11th R. Dublin Fus: B.	
"	19/4/17	a.m	Inspected the transport of 7th (S.I.H) Batn: Rgt. and gave lecture & demonstration of route for respirators for drivers.	
"	"	p.m	Inspected 144th & 145th Co. R.E. & 148th Ind: Train	
"	20/4/17	a.m	Inspected 47th Motor Veh: Sectn.	
"	"	p.m	Inspected 156th Co R.E.	
"	21/4/17	a.m	Inspected B/Batt 75/Batt 177th Bde R.F.A.	
"	"	p.m	Inspected 111th Field Ambulance. 157th Co R.E.	
"	22/4/17	a.m	Inspected 11th Hants. 47th Infy Bde Hd.qrs.	
"	23/4/17	a.m	Inspected 47th Motor Veh: Sectn. Closed advanced Veh: Aid Post at Judas Copse. St Ledger.	
"	"	p.m	Inspected 49th Machine Gun Co. & 157th Co R.E. Received wire from ADVS VI Corps that Lieut. L.P. Right AVC has received orders to proceed from No 2 V.H. to 16th Div	
"	24/4/17	a.m	Attended Conference at office of ADVS VI Corps Headquarters	

WAR DIARY / INTELLIGENCE SUMMARY

Army Form C. 2118.

Place	Date	Hour	Summary of Events and Information	Remarks and references to Appendices
Behagnies	25/10/17	am	Inspected Hqrs Signal Co. & 118th Field Ambulance	
"	26/11/17	am	Inspected 47th Mobile Vety Section	
			Lieut Leslie Penrhys Pugh A.V.C. reported today for duty with this division	
"	27/11/17	am	Inspected 10th R. Dublins. 2nd R. Irish Regt and 48th Inf Bde Headquarters.	
"	28/11/17	am	Inspected B & C Batteries 177th Bde R.F.A.	
		pm	Inspected A/Bty. 160th 173rd Bde R.F.A.	
"	29/11/17	am	Inspected Hqrs of 107th Divisional Headquarters M.M.P. hrs & 16th Divl Signal Co.	
"	30/11/17	am	Inspected the horses men and all equipment of 47th M.V. Section	
		pm	Conference 1.P.03	

Brennan DeLure
Major
DADVS 16th Divn

WAR DIARY,

FOR MONTH OF DECEMBER, 1917.

VOLUME :- 25.

UNIT :- D.A.D.V.S. 16th Division

WAR DIARY or INTELLIGENCE SUMMARY

Army Form C. 2118.

DADVS 16th Division

Place	Date	Hour	Summary of Events and Information	Remarks and references to Appendices
Béhagnies	1/12/17	a.m.	Attended Conference of ADVS & Officer VI Corps	
	2/12/17	a.m.	Inspected ⅓ horse trucks & 180th Bde R.F.A.	
		p.m.	" " " 177th Bde R.F.A.	
Ytres	3/12/17	a.m.	16th Divl Headquarters removed to Ytres – & I Corps area	
Ytres	4/12/17		Reported to ADVS VI Corps	
Ytres	5/12/17		Obtained billet for 47th M.V. Section at Flavicourt	
Flavicourt	6/12/17		16th Divl Headquarters moved to Flavicourt ½ mile west of Péronne and into VII Corps area.	
"	5/12/17		Arranged with O.C. 1/1 Lancashire M.V.S. 53rd Divn to move 47 mob V.S. to the same billet at Villers Faucon	
"	6/12/17		Visited 47th M.V.S. at Villers Faucon	
Villers Faucon	7/12/17		16th Divl Headquarters moved to Villers Faucon. Reported to ADVS VII Corps. E.2.6. A. map 62.C. France. Capt Len 16D1 A.V.C. O.C. 47th Mob Vet Section. Granted leave to Canada. Capt Cawthorn appointed O.C. 47 Mob Vet Section.	

WAR DIARY
or
INTELLIGENCE SUMMARY.
(Erase heading not required.)

Army Form C. 2118.

(2)

Place	Date	Hour	Summary of Events and Information	Remarks and references to Appendices
VillersFaucon	8/12/17	a.m	Attended Conference of Officers of A.D.M.S VII Corps H.Qrs.	
"	9/12/17	a	Inspected 7th Remounts	
"	"	p	Inspected 47 M.S. Vet. Section. Inspected the horses at 46 H. Artry Bde H.Qrs.	
"	10/12/17	am	Inspected the horses and mules of 111th Hants.	
"	"	pm	Inspected 11 - 157 It Co R.E.	
"	11/12/17	am	Inspected 2nd & 2/9 R Dublin Fus. mapr Lees	
"	"	pm	Inspected the mapr lions & 164 & 110 It & 48th Infy Bde H.Qrs.	
"	12/12/17	am	Inspected the mapr lions & 2nd R Ind Regt. 7/6 R I Fus	
"	"	1pm	4th (S.I.H) R Lucel Regt. 7/6 Inns In.	
"	"	pm	Inspected 47 46 mobile vety Sec	
"	13/12/17	"	Inspected 143. 144. 145. Cos & 16 Divl Train	
"	14/12/17	"	Inspected 155 & 156 Cos R.E.	
"	"	am	Conference p.O at officers of A.D.M.S VII Corps	
"	"	pm	Attended Conference of officers of A.D.M.S VII Corps	
"	15/12/17	am	Inspected 47 H.mobile Vety Section	

Army Form C. 2118.

WAR DIARY
or
INTELLIGENCE SUMMARY.
(3.)
(Erase heading not required.)

Place	Date	Hour	Summary of Events and Information	Remarks and references to Appendices
Villers Faucon	18/12/17	a.m.	Inspected 11th Tanks and 757th T.O.R.K.	
"	1/1/18	a.m.	Inspected 47th Mobile Vety Section 16/12/17 to 31/12/17. Officers in leave to U.K. Brennan Dillon Major A.V.C. DADVS 16th Division	

Vol 26

WAR DIARY,

FOR MONTH OF JANUARY, 1918.

VOLUME :- 26

UNIT :- DaDVS. 16 Division

WAR DIARY BY DADVS
INTELLIGENCE SUMMARY

16th Ind. Division

Army Form C. 2118.

(Erase heading not required.)

Place	Date	Hour	Summary of Events and Information	Remarks and references to Appendices
Villers=Faucon	1/1/18		Inspected the horses of 111th Field Ambulance.	
"	2/1/18	am	Inspected the lines of Divisional Headquarters - Police & Signal Co.	
"	"	pm	Inspected 11th Hants.	
"	3/1/18	a	Inspected the 47th M.V.S. and transport lines 48th Infy Bde.	
"	"	pm	Inspected 156th & 157th Co. R.E.	
"	4/1/18	am	Inspected the horses of 147th & 49th Infy Bdes	
"	"	pm	Inspected 155th Co. R.E.	
"	5/1/18	am	Attended conference at Offices ADVS VII Corps Headquarters	
"	6/1/18	"	Inspected the lines of 143, 144 & 145 Cos 16th Field Ambce A.S.C.	
"	7/1/18	am	Inspected 160th Bde R.F.A. sent to M.V.S. for treatment on case of Ophthalmia	
"	"		Inspected 177th Bde R.F.A.	
"	9/1/18	am	Inspected 156th Co. R.E. and 113th Field Ambulance	
"	9/1/18	pm	Inspected 16th D.A.C. and 112th Field Ambulance	

WAR DIARY or INTELLIGENCE SUMMARY.

Army Form C. 2118.

Place	Date	Hour	Summary of Events and Information	Remarks and references to Appendices
VILLERS FAUCON	11/1/18		Inspected 1st/1st Munster, 7th Royal Irish Rifles & 47th MVS	
"	12/1/18		Inspected 48th & 49th Machine Gun Co and 111th Field Ambulance. Attended Conference at VII Corps H.Qrs. Remounts before being warned.	
"	13/1/18		Inspected 46th Division by the Division. Inspected 47th Machine Gun Co.	
"	14/1/18		Inspected 16th Div Sam A.S.C. and the 49th Infy Bd. Inspected TC 47th M.V.S. to send all NCO's & men. 6/13th Field Ambulance for medical Examination and Classification in Category A or B	
"	15/1/18		All A.V.C. Sgt Mervere sent 6/13 to 70 Amb for Chiropody in category A or B. Inspected 160th Bde R.F.A.	
"	16/1/18		Inspected 47 M.V.S. "K Hunks' & 13th Co R.E. 49th Infy Bd Headquarters.	

Army Form C. 2118.

WAR DIARY
or
INTELLIGENCE SUMMARY.

(3)

(Erase heading not required.)

Instructions regarding War Diaries and Intelligence Summaries are contained in F. S. Regs., Part II. and the Staff Manual respectively. Title pages will be prepared in manuscript.

Place	Date	Hour	Summary of Events and Information	Remarks and references to Appendices
VILLERS FAUCON	17/1/18	am	Inspected the M.M.P. horses. 15.6th C. R.E.	
		pm	Inspected HQ Coy 16th DAC	
	18.1.18	am	Inspected 157th C.R.E. 49th M.V.S.	
		pm	Inspected the 1st R. Munsters.	
	19/1/18	am	Inspected the 269th Machine Gun Co. which have arrived from England and are attached to 16th Divn. arrangements have the horses malleined on 21st. Attended Conference 15 U.R.	
			6th Connaught Rangers	
~	20/1/18		Capt Cawthorn O.C. 47th M.V.S. returns from leave U.K.	
			Inspected 47th Mobile Veterinary section	
	21/1/18		Inspected 49th Infty Bde transport lines.	
			Capt Rees V.O. to 49th Infty Bde proceeded on leave to U.K.	
			16th Divl Headquarters moved to J.17.B.8.8. ½ mile	
TINCOURT.	22.1.18		N.W. TINCOURT. Map 62.C. 1.40,000.	
			Inspected 269th MGC Coy's horses.	
~	23/1/18		Inspected 269th MG Coy & all MG horses malleined on 21st.	
			passed – no reactors.	

WAR DIARY
or
INTELLIGENCE SUMMARY.
(Erase heading not required.)

Army Form C. 2118.

Place	Date	Hour	Summary of Events and Information	Remarks and references to Appendices
TINCOURT	24-1-18		Inspected Uniforms of 16th Divl Headquarters. 111th Field Ambulance. Forwarded A.V.C. Records against final A.V.C. med. returns 16th divn showing Chiefly Cat. A.19 Category B. 18.-	
"	25-1-18		Inspected 177th Bde R.F.A.	
"	26-1-18		Inspected 180th Bde R.F.A. & 11th Hants	
"	27-1-18		Inspected M.M. Platoons & 48th M.G. Coy	
"	28-1-18		Inspected 6th Connaught 2nd & 1st Rn Irish Rifles 7 Roy Irish Rifles + 1st Munsters	
"	29-1-18		Inspected Nos 2 & 3 Sections 16th D.A.C.	
"	30-1/18		Inspected at La Chapellette station 64 remounts which arrived for 16th Division. These three animals were found affected with Strangles.	
"	31/1/18		Inspected 56th Infy Bde HQrs. 1st 2nd and 10th R. Dublin Fus. Pneumonia Deliriums Major Brennan MSDVS 16th Division. 1/2/18	

WAR DIARY By DADVS
or
INTELLIGENCE SUMMARY. 16th Division

Army Form C. 2118.

Place	Date	Hour	Summary of Events and Information	Remarks and references to Appendices
ANCOURT	1/2/18	am	Inspected 48th and 49th Machine Gun Co.	
"	2/2/16	pm	Conference of Vety Officers at Offices of A.D.V.S.	
			Inspected the transport animals of 2nd Leinster Regt. which arrived from 24th Division	
"	3/2/18	pm	Inspected the 47th Mob Vety Section	
"	4/2/18	am	Inspected 49th Infy Bde transport animals	
			Inspected the transport animals of 2nd Munsters Regt which arrived from 1st Division to join the 48th Infy Bde	
		pm	Inspected the animals awaiting evacuation at 47th Mobile Vety Sec	
"	5/2/18	am	Inspected 177th Bde R.F.A.	
		pm	Inspected 34 horses of 277 Bde A.F.A. supply ech. attached from to day to 16th Div Train.	
"	6/2/18		In company of A.D.V.S. VII Corps inspected 180th Bde R.F.A. — In morning 26th mve field supplies at Beaumetz	

WAR DIARY
INTELLIGENCE SUMMARY

Army Form C. 2118.

(4)

Place	Date	Hour	Summary of Events and Information	Remarks and references to Appendices
TINCOURT	20-2-18	a.m.	Inspected the Transport animals of 2nd R. Irish Regt.	
"	21/2/18	p.m.	Inspected the 16th Divl. Train horses.	
"		a.m.	Inspected the horses/mules of 16th D.A.C.	
"		p.m.	Inspected the transport animals 7/16 Bn. R. Innis. Fus.	
"	22/2/18	a.m.	Attended Conference of D.A.D.V.S. of VII Corps at T.P.O.	
"		–	Recieved. Tetanus	
"	23/2/18	a.m.	Inspected the horses & mules of 111th Field Ambulance	
"			Inspected 112 & 113 H.Q. Ambulances.	
"			Inspected 47 & 71 MGC	
"		p.m.	Inspected 47 & 71 Mac Gun Co.	
"	24/2/16	a.m.	Inspected the horses of 1st & 2nd R. Munster Fus.	
"	25/2/18	a.m.	Inspected the horses awaiting Evacuation at 47 M.V.S.	
"		p.m.	Inspected the horses & mules 1 B. Batt. 160 & Bde R.F.A.	
"	26/2/18	a.m.	Inspected to 2 Section 16 Bn D.A.C.	
"	27/2/18	–	Inspected the R.E. horses attached 272, 43bde A.F.A.	
"	28/2/18	–	German animals awaiting Evacuation. Brennan Dellwin Major	
			D.A.D.V.S. 16th Division.	

Army Form C. 2118.

WAR DIARY
or
INTELLIGENCE SUMMARY.
(Erase heading not required.)

(2)

Instructions regarding War Diaries and Intelligence Summaries are contained in F.S. Regs., Part II. and the Staff Manual respectively. Title pages will be prepared in manuscript.

Place	Date	Hour	Summary of Events and Information	Remarks and references to Appendices
Fincourt	11-3-18		Inspected the horses & mules machinery & ammunition at 47th Mid Vety Section	
"	12-3-18		Inspected the transport of 16th Divl Signal Co & 48th Machine Gun Co.	
"	13/3/18		Inspected the horses & transport of 16th D.A.C. Inspected 7th R. Irish Regt and 2nd Dublins	
"	14/3/18		Inspection the transport of 155th & 156th Co RE and 113th Field Ambulance	
			Major Genl Hull. K.C.B. G.O.C. 16th Divn inspected 47th Mobile Vety Section.	
"	15/3/18		Inspected the transport 46th My Bde.	
"	16/3/18		Attended Conference at office of A.D.V.S. W. Corps. D.D.V.S. Fifth Army inspected 47th Mobile Vety Sectn.	
"	17/3/18		Inspection horses & mules of 180th Bde R.F.A.	
"	18/3/18		Inspected horses & mules of 177th Bde R.F.A.	

WAR DIARY
INTELLIGENCE SUMMARY

Army Form C. 2118.

(3)

Place	Date	Hour	Summary of Events and Information	Remarks and references to Appendices
VINCOURT	19-3-18		Inspected the lines & works of 16th Divl Signal Coy S.L.I. 7th R Innis Rifles	
"	20/3/18		Inspected 47th Infy Bde Transport.	
	21/3/18		Inspected 47th Mobile Vety Section. Gave instructions to O.C. 47 M.V.S. to move to PERONNE on 22/3/18	
DOINGT	22/3/18		16 to Divl Headquarters removed to DOINGT 1 mile E of PERONNE. Inspected horses to Infy Bdes behind in the trench at DOINGT.	
BIACHES	23/3/18		16 to Divl Headquarters moved to BIACHES at 7 am and now from BIACHES to CAPPY at 3 PM	
CAPPY	24/3/18		16 to Divl Headquarters moved to MORCOURT	
MORLANCOURT	25/3/18		16 to Divl Headquarters moved to LAMOTTE Inspected 16 D.A.C.	
LAMOTTE	26/3/18		16 Divl Headquarters moved to PETIT BLANGY	
PETIT BLANGY	27/3/18		Inspected 16 to Divl Train transport. Inspected 177 to Bde R.F.A.	

WAR DIARY
or
INTELLIGENCE SUMMARY.

Army Form C. 2118.

(*Erase heading not required.*)

Place	Date	Hour	Summary of Events and Information	Remarks and references to Appendices
Petit Blangy	28/3/16		Inspected 160 to Bde RFA. Rotary with R.T.O. to Incrate train for SALEUX.	
"	29/3/16		Inspected transport 2 y g & Infy Bde	
"	30/3/16		Inspected 155, 156 & Co RE	
"	31/3/16		Inspected 11 H. Hants & 157 & Co RE	
	1/4/16.			

Brennan Dullin
Major
D.A.D.V.S.
16th Divn

WAR DIARY
INTELLIGENCE SUMMARY.
(Erase heading not required.)

Army Form C. 2118.

(2)

Place	Date	Hour	Summary of Events and Information	Remarks and references to Appendices
FAUQUEM-BERGUES	11/4/18		Inspected 143 & 144 (6.A.S.C.) 16th Div'l Train	
FAUQUEMBERQUES	11/4/18		Aus 5. 113th Field Ambulance	
	12/4/18		Interviewed A.D.V.S. XIII Corps — Inspected 111th	
			& 112th Field Ambulances	
	12/4/18		Inspected 16th D.A.C. attached 51st Div.	
	14/4/18		Inspected horse + mule lines Remainder	
			at 47th M.V.S.	
	15/4/18		16th Div'l Headquarters moved from Fauquembergues	
			to AIRE	
AIRE	16/4/18		Interviewed 16 Senr V.O. 7C. 1st Polygon Bde	
			attached 16th Div.	
	17/4/18		Inspected 111th Field Ambulance & 143 — To A.S.C.	
	18/4/18		Inspected 112th field Ambulance + 144 — T. A.S.C.	
	19/4/18		9th Rifle Brig. Lent R.E. 2nd Dembles transport	
			Inspected h- 1st R. Munst. transport Forms	
	20/4/18		& then M.M. 16 – 5 J. Division	

WAR DIARY
INTELLIGENCE SUMMARY

(3)

Army Form C. 2118.

Place	Date	Hour	Summary of Events and Information	Remarks and references to Appendices
AIRE	21/4/18		Inspected H. Transport M.M. Tanks & 142 COAVC	
"	22/4/18		Inspected the horses and mules of 16th D.A.C.	
"	23/4/18		Inspected 16th Signal Co. horses & mules - Interviewed ADVS at Corps H.Q.	
"	24/4/18		Inspected the horses & mules of 1st Dragoons & 17th Rsrs.	
"	25/4/18		Inspected the horses & mules of 4th Co. R.E. & Porhyjers	
			Interviewed Alexander DDVS 2nd Army & Vet Cochrane	
			ADVS 11th Corps at 47 A.Mob.Vy.Sectn.	
	26/4/18		DADVS left for 14 days special leave to U.K.	

B. Numan D? Vm Majr
ADVS
16th Division

WAR DIARY
INTELLIGENCE SUMMARY

Army Form C. 2118.

DADMS 16th Division

Vol 30

Place	Date	Hour	Summary of Events and Information	Remarks and references to Appendices
AIRE	10/5/18		DADMS returned from leave to U.K.	
"	11/5/18		Inspected the horse transport of 112th Field Ambulance. 112th Field Ambulance are attached 61st Division after 27th American Division.	
"	12/5/18		In company with ADMS 11th Corps inspected 49th Infy Bde. 111th Field Ambulance & 144 Co. A.S.C. (16th Train)	
"	13/5/18		In company with ADMS 11th Corps inspected 47 & 7-48 Infy Bde movement & 113 to field Ambulances	
"	14/5/18		Inspected first Infy Bde Polygon attacks 16 Div.	
"	15/5/18		16th Division moved from Aire to Camp 6.R. 9 units S.E. of BOULOGNE	
SAMER	16/5/18		Inspected 2nd R. Dublin Fusrs & 2nd R. Munster	
"	17/5/18		Inspected H.Qrs Signal Co. & 1 M.M. Platoon	
"	18/5/18		Inspected 144 11115 Co. A.S.C. 16th Train	

WAR DIARY
or
INTELLIGENCE SUMMARY.
(Erase heading not required.)

Army Form C. 2118.

Place	Date	Hour	Summary of Events and Information	Remarks and references to Appendices
SAMER	19/5/18		The 1st Time transferred to 2nd R. Dublin Fus. hereby say to 2nd Batt. 59th Infy Regt. U.S.A. and the 70th Inf. Brigade 2nd R. Munster Fuseliers landed over to 3rd Batt 59 Inf. Regt. U.S.A.	
"	20/5/18		Inspected 4/7th Batt A.P. 6th Conn. Regt. & 118th Mach Gun Batt.	
"	21/5/18		Inspected remounts at 148 Co. R.S.C.	
"	22/5/18		Company with Sous Lieutenants 4th American Div. inspected 60 horses which were very lean. U.S.A. Div.	
"	23/5/18		Interview B.D.V.S. First Army — Arrays to forward A.D.O.S. of 4th Div. U.S.A. through this office.	
"	24/5/18		Inspected 47 mob. Vet. section & 118th Field Ambulance sections the Vety officers of 4th American Division on the complete of 4 AP.C. Laborers.	
"	25/5/18		Inspected 143, 144, Co. A.S.C. & 118th Field Ambs 4th U.S.A. Mob. Vet. Sect. at Arranged a billet for 4th U.S.A. Mob. Vet. Sect. at WIERRE-AU-BOIS.	

WAR DIARY
INTELLIGENCE SUMMARY

Army Form C. 2118.

(3)

(Erase heading not required.)

Place	Date	Hour	Summary of Events and Information	Remarks and references to Appendices
Cam. G.R.	26/5/18		Inspected 158 Remounts being handed over to 4th American Division	
—	27/5/18		In company with V.O's of 4th USA trm inspected the horses of 1st Regt Engineers & 39th Infy Regt.	
—	28/5/18		Inspected 48th & 59th Infy Bde HQrs & station of gns & munitions	
—	29/5/18		Inspected 6 to Coms & pts to HQrs & 47 to Infy Bde HQrs	
—	30/5/18		Reconnaissance - hauled Veterinary Officers of 4th USA Division visited the 10th, 12th, 13th Vety Hospitals and No 3 Horse Convol Depot.	
—	31/5/18		Inspected 11th Hussars, 49th Infy Bde HQrs.	

Behrmann Esthr
Major A.V.C.

DADVS 16th Division

WAR DIARY by DADVS 16th Division
INTELLIGENCE SUMMARY.
(Erase heading not required.)

Army Form C. 2118.

Vol 31

Place	Date	Hour	Summary of Events and Information	Remarks and references to Appendices
SAMER	1/6/18		In Company with Sen Veterinarian inspected 39 & 39th Mec Gun Co. 4th American Division — Inspected Equipment 847th Mobile Vety Sectin	
"	2/6/18		Inspected one hundred remounts which are being issued to 4th American Division —	
"	3/6/18		Inspected the transport animals of 16th Div. Rangers. Inspected the horses & mules of 135 & 2nd Co RE — and 135th Field Ambulance — The 4th American Mobile Vety Section arrived at SAMGR & attached to 747 Mobile Vety Section for instruction.	
"	4/6/18		Vety officers 4th American Divi instructed in the flying of U.S.A FA 3000	
"	5/6/18		Inspected Signal Co 16th Div. 4th U.S.A. Mobile Veterinary Section — Discussed D.D.R. Sick army horse remounts to 4th American M.V.S.	

WAR DIARY
or
INTELLIGENCE SUMMARY.
(Erase heading not required.)

Army Form C. 2118.

Place	Date	Hour	Summary of Events and Information	Remarks and references to Appendices
SAMER	6/6/18		Inspected 136th Cy Ambulance & 6th Devon Regt & Cyclists Signal Co Transport and Div HSpo Transport	
"	8/6/18		Inspected the transport of 11 Hants, 7th Royal Irish Regt 49 HSp & HSpo	
"	9/6/18		Company with Senr Veterinarian inspected the transport of 4th American division.	
"	10/6/18		Lieut Pugh AVC granted 14 days leave to England Inspected HT to Motor Vetry Section	
"	11/6/18		Inspected the horse 2 mules of 144 Co RFC 60th American division HSpo. Same were Major Jewell Senr Veterinant reported to this officer	
"	12/6/18		Inspected the transport of 13 HSp Ambulance and 48 HBa HSpo	
"	13/6/18		Inspected the horses of 143 Co ACC & 4) 136 HSpo and 16 Divl HSpo	

Army Form C. 2118.

WAR DIARY
or
INTELLIGENCE SUMMARY.
(Erase heading not required.)

(3)

Instructions regarding War Diaries and Intelligence Summaries are contained in F. S. Regs., Part II. and the Staff Manual respectively. Title pages will be prepared in manuscript.

Place	Date	Hour	Summary of Events and Information	Remarks and references to Appendices
SAMER	14/6/16		Interviewed all the Vety Officers of 80th Divn. U.S.A. afternoon	
"	15/6/16		Inspected the horses of 135 D. Amm. & 145 Co A.S.C.	
"	16/6/16		Interviewed D.D.V.S. First Army — Received orders to proceed to England with 16 Vet. Remy Staff	
Boulogne	17/6/16		16th Division moved to Boulogne	
"	18/6/16		16 Division embarked at Boulogne returned to Folkestone	
		6 pm	Steamer landed at Folkestone & proceeded Aldershot	
ALDERSHOT	19/6/16	2 am	19/6/16 — Proceeded to Bordley Camp	
"	20/6/16		Interviewed Camp Commandant & inspected detached units for transport	
"			Interviewed P.C. Remount depot	
"	23/4/16		DADVS on leave 22/6/16 to 25/6/16	
"	24/6/16		Inspected 196 Remounts for No 2 Sec 16 D.A.C. Interviewed D.D.V.S. Aldershot Command	
"	27/6/16		V. Murrey Capt Vety Hospital & arranged for successive jay sick	

A6945 Wt. W14422/M160 350,000 12/16 D.D.&L. Forms/C.2118/14.

WAR DIARY
or
INTELLIGENCE SUMMARY.
(Erase heading not required.)

Army Form C. 2118.

(4)

Place	Date	Hour	Summary of Events and Information	Remarks and references to Appendices
BOURLEY CAMP ALDERSHOT	28/4/16		Inspected 3's Remounts for 14 December Received 11 (25lb) Vety Field Chests & One Vety Medicine for A.V.C. Est. Army D.O.V's instructions Freeman.	
	29/4/16		Inspected 5's Remounts for 3/4 & 5 Gordons	
	30/4/16		Inspected 3's Remounts for 11th R. Scot. Fus. Inspected 3's Remounts ful 11 R. Irish Fus.	

Brennan D.V.in
Major A/C
DADVS 16th Div.

30/4/16.

WAR DIARY By DADVS 16th Division Army Form C. 2118.
or
INTELLIGENCE SUMMARY.
(Erase heading not required.)

Place	Date	Hour	Summary of Events and Information	Remarks and references to Appendices
SAMER.	1/8/18		Arrived at Desvres at 1 P.M. by train from HAVRE. Travelled in Company with 49th Infy Bde Transport — Detrained at DESVRES and proceeded to SAMER. — 49th Bde Infy Transport proceeded by road to PARENTY.	
"	2-8-18		Inspected the transport 16th Divl Hqrs + 447th Mobile Vety Sectn + 447o Signal Co.	
"	3-8-18 am		Inspected 447th Mobile Vety Sectn - 142 C.A.S.C.	
"	" pm		Inspected 16th Machine Gun Battn.	
"	4/5/8/18		In company with 6 R.E. Standing inspected 157th R.E.	
"	5/8/18 am		Inspected 11th Hants (P) Transport.	
"	" pm		Inspected 15·S·H·Co + 115·G·Co·R.E.	
"	6-8-18 am		Inspected 49th Infy Bde Hqrs Transport — 34th London Co. Son D.D.&.T. Supt Coy + 10th Flack transport.	

WAR DIARY or INTELLIGENCE SUMMARY

Army Form C. 2118.

Place	Date	Hour	Summary of Events and Information	Remarks and references to Appendices
SAMER	7-5-18	am	Inspected 143rd Co. A.S.C. 48th Infy. Bde M/g transport	
		pm	Inspected the transport animals of 19th Northumberland Fusiliers, 18 Scottish Rifles & 11th Royal Scots Fusiliers.	
"	8-5-18	am	Inspected the 144th Co. A.S.C.	
"		pm	Inspected the transport of 47th Bn M/Gs, 9th Royal Highlanders and 7th Wellesley's.	
"	9-5-18	am	Inspected 145th Co. A.S.C. 143 S.A.A. sec. D.A.C.	
	10-5-18		Inspected 147 Co. A.S.C.	
	11-5-18	am	Inspected the transport of M.T.S. transport 112th Fd. Ambulance	
		pm	Inspection the transport of 77th Field Ambulance	
"	12-5-18	pm	Lecture at 2 pm on Annual management of DADVS at 49th Infantry Bde H.Q. PARENTY	
			Inspected transport of 157th Co R.E.	

Army Form C. 2118.

WAR DIARY by DADMS
or
INTELLIGENCE SUMMARY. 16th Div.

(Erase heading not required.)

(3)

Place	Date	Hour	Summary of Events and Information	Remarks and references to Appendices
SAMER	13-8-18	a.m.	Inspected the horse-ponies of 16th Div. HQrs.	
"		p.m.	Lecture on Horse Management by DADVS at 2 p.m. at 47th Infy Bde Headquarters	
"	14-8-18	a.m.	Inspected the transport animals of 16 to 22nd Signal Co	
"		p.m.	Lecture by DADVS on Horse Management at 48th Infy Bde Headquarters — DesIRES.	
"	15-8-18	a.m.	Inspected the transport of 15th Scottish Rifles	
"		p.m.	attended Signal Co Horse Show at 5 p.m. E.P.	
"	16-8-18	a.m.	Inspected the horses & mules of SAA section 16 DAC	
"		p.m.	attended D.A.C. Horse Show.	
"	17-8-18	a.m.	attended 49th Infy Bde Horse Show.	
"		p.m.	Capt C. G. Mahon OC 47 MVS proceeded on leave to Sy low.	

Army Form C. 2118.

WAR DIARY
or
INTELLIGENCE SUMMARY
(Erase heading not required.)

Place	Date	Hour	Summary of Events and Information	Remarks and references to Appendices
SAMER	18.8.18		Lieut/Capt Ray A.V.C. I/c of 47 A.T.M.V.S. during Capt. Cawthorn's absence. Received warning notice that the Division would move on Monday. 19th for the 47th M.V.S. to move on 19 hour on Company with 49th Bde M.V.S.	
Monchy Cayeux	19.8.18		164 Inf. Headquarters left Samer and proceeded to MONCHY CAYEUX. Inspected 7 & 9th Bde transport on arrival at ANVIN at 6 p.m. 4) Mobile Vet Sec arriving at Monchy Cayeux -	
"	21.8.18		Inspected 7 & 7th Bde transport at ANVIN on their arrival.	

Army Form C. 2118.

WAR DIARY
or
INTELLIGENCE SUMMARY.
(Erase heading not required.)

(5)

Instructions regarding War Diaries and Intelligence Summaries are contained in F. S. Regs., Part II. and the Staff Manual respectively. Title pages will be prepared in manuscript.

Place	Date	Hour	Summary of Events and Information	Remarks and references to Appendices
Monchy Cayeux	22.8.16		16th Div. Headquarters left Monchy CAYEUX and arrived at Ruitz at 2. p.m.	
Ruitz	23.8.16		Reported personnel at Office M.A.D.V.S. I Corps HQrs. — Inspected 16th Mac Gun Bath at BARLIN.	
	24.8.16 a.m.		Inspected 143 2nd & 144 2nd Cos A.S.C. transport	
		p.m.	Inspected 47th M.V.S. at BARLIN.	
	25.8.16		Inspected the horses & mules of 147 is Bde R.F.A. attached 16th Divn ————	
	26.8.16		Inspected 4.5th Inf Bde transport at MONT Beauchamp at LES MINES	

WAR DIARY
or
INTELLIGENCE SUMMARY

Army Form C. 2118.

Place	Date	Hour	Summary of Events and Information	Remarks and references to Appendices
Ruits	27-9-16	a.m.	Inspected 4.9th Infantry Bde. Transport	
	"	p.m.	Inspected the transport 155 & 156 Coys R.E.	
	28-9-16	a.m.	Inspected the transport 11th & 12th Fus.	
			Ambulances	
	"	p.m.	Inspects the transport 11th Hack (?)	
			Inspects 47th M.T.J.	
	29-9-16		Icontam into A.D.V.S. I Corps before	
			the 11th Field Ambulance & 47th Inf Bde & 19/6 mmth Machine	
	30-9-16	a.m.	Inspects 16th Hrse gun Bde & 19/6 mmth Machine Gun	
	"		into min 1st D.V.S. at 47th M.V.S	
	"	p.m.	Inspect S.A.A. 16th D.A.C	

Army Form C. 2118.

WAR DIARY
or
INTELLIGENCE SUMMARY.
(Erase heading not required.)

Instructions regarding War Diaries and Intelligence Summaries are contained in F. S. Regs., Part II. and the Staff Manual respectively. Title pages will be prepared in manuscript.

(7)

Place	Date	Hour	Summary of Events and Information	Remarks and references to Appendices
Ruitz	31-8-16		Inspection home to building 16th Bnd Headquarters M.M.P. & R.E. Head quarters.	

Brennan DeVine
Major.
D A D V S.
16th Division.

31/8/16.

WAR DIARY by DADVS

INTELLIGENCE SUMMARY. 16th Division

Army Form C. 2118.

Vol 34

Place	Date	Hour	Summary of Events and Information	Remarks and references to Appendices
Ruitz	1-9-18	a.m.	Inspected the transport & Horses of 47 Mob Vet Section reported his return from leave in England. Capt Osborn D.C.	
		p.m.	Inspected the transport animals of 16th Signal Co	
"	2-9-18	a.m.	Inspected HQrs & 16 Divl train at ARRA. Inspected the horse standards of 177 Bde RFA & 16st B & RFA (16 Divl Artilly) attached XXII Corps.	
		"	Inspected 16th D.A.C. attd XIII Corps	
		"	A.D.V.S. I Corps called at 7.30 pm dispatched to him the condition of the Artillery animals inspected today.	
	3-9-18	a.m.	Inspected the transport animals of 22nd Northumberland Fus & Bath Bdn.	
"		p.m.	Inspected the transport & a 1st Royal Highlanders 47th Lgt Bde	

WAR DIARY

INTELLIGENCE SUMMARY

(Erase heading not required.)

Army Form C. 2118.

Place	Date	Hour	Summary of Events and Information	Remarks and references to Appendices
Ruitz	4.9.18	a.m.	Inspected the transport of 156th and 157th Co. R.E.	
"	"	p.m.	Inspected the transport of 16th Machine Gun Batt'n.	
"	5-9-18	a.m.	Inspected the transport of 153rd Co. R.E. + 49th Infy Bde Wagons	
"	"	p.m.	Inspected the horse + mules of A. Vet. Hosp., Police, & C.R.E.	
"	6-9-18	a.m.	D.A.D.V.S. attended at the lines of 19th N'thumberland Fus. & others on a horse judging competition.	
"	"	p.m.	Inspected the transport of 11th Div'l Signal Co.	
"	7-9-18	a.m.	Inspected No. 1, 2, & 3 sections 16 M.A.C.	
"	—	p.m.	In company with A.D.V.S. Army, inspected the transport of 4 & 75th 49th Infy Bde.	
"	8-9-18	a.m.	Inspected the transport of 177th Bde R.F.A.	
"	9-9-18	a.m.	Inspected 47th Mobile Vet. Sec'n.	

WAR DIARY or INTELLIGENCE SUMMARY

Army Form C. 2118.

Place	Date	Hour	Summary of Events and Information	Remarks and references to Appendices
Ruitz	9-9-18	p.m.	Inspected Ammunition of A & B Batteries 180 Nth RFA	
	10-9-18	a.m.	Inspected A & B Batteries 180th Bde R.F.A.	
		p.m.	Inspected C & D Batteries 180th Bde. and 15th Trench Mortar Battery	
	11-9-18	a.m.	Inspected 177th Bde R.F.A.	
	12-9-18	a.m.	Examined 31 Remounts received from 7th Div	
			Conference re No kill at Ypres of DADVS A/ANVS I Corps called at Office	
		p.m.	Capt Luckings V.O. 70 177 & 73 Bde R.F.A. left for 14 days leave to UK	
	13-9-18		Divisional Gas. & D.V.S. visited 47th Mot. Battie. Inspected 133 Co R.E. transport	

Army Form C. 2118.

WAR DIARY
or
INTELLIGENCE SUMMARY
(Erase heading not required.)

(4)

Place	Date	Hour	Summary of Events and Information	Remarks and references to Appendices
Rui[3]	14-9-18		Inspected the transport of 1/6th Somerset Light Infy, 16 Stg Bde and 3/4 London. Received an application from the D.V.S. for a confidential report on Capt MacArthur and Lieut MacLeod both attached to 4th Division U.S.A. forwarded report.	
"	15-9-18	a.m.	Inspected 105 Remounts arrived from Calais for issue to R.F.A. 16th Division. —	
		p.m.	Inspected the transport of 4 & 6th Infy Reinforcements.	
	16-9-18	a.m.	Inspected 47 # Mobile Vety Section.	
		p.m.	Inspected the transport of 4/7th Infy Reinforcements and the horses of M.M.P.	

Army Form C. 2118.

WAR DIARY
or
INTELLIGENCE SUMMARY
(Erase heading not required.)

Place	Date	Hour	Summary of Events and Information	Remarks and references to Appendices
Ruitz	17-9-18	am	I Corps Horse Show at BARLIN. Inspected the Horses. 19th Mob Lamdries before dispersal —	
"	18-9-18		Inspected 1 ADS & Signal Co here...	
"	19-9-18		Inspected Ph horses & mules of 180 "73rd R.F.A. Inspected 47 #M.V.S. & 16th Machine Gun Batt transport -	
"	20-9-18		Inspected 9/7 Infy & Bde - Inspected the transport -	
"	21-9-18		Inspected Ch Chargis & transport animals of 1st to 2nd Hampshire. Recd Orders BGC 47 #M.V.S. to move from BARLIN to DROUVIN on 22/9/18	
"			Routine	

Army Form C. 2118.

WAR DIARY By DADVS
or
INTELLIGENCE SUMMARY. 16th Division
(Erase heading not required.)

Instructions regarding War Diaries and Intelligence Summaries are contained in F. S. Regs., Part II. and the Staff Manual respectively. Title pages will be prepared in manuscript.

Place	Date	Hour	Summary of Events and Information	Remarks and references to Appendices
DROUVIN	1/10/18	am	Inspected 16 Dvl Mobile Veterinary Section. 16 Dvl Squadron Horses	
		pm	Inspects 1/4 Hampshires — 11th Tanks —	
	2/10/18	am	In Company with ADVS. I Corps — inspects 46th + 49th Divs	
			Btns Hampshire.	
		pm	Inspects 177th + 160th Bdes RFA	
	3/10/18	am	Inspects 157th Coy RE.	
		pm	Inspects 16th Machine Gun Bat. —	
	4/10/18	am	Inspects. 16 Dvl Train.	
	5/10/18	am	Inspects No 1 Sechn 16 DAC	
	6/10/18		Inspects 155th + 156th Coy RE.	

Army Form C. 2118.

WAR DIARY
or
INTELLIGENCE SUMMARY.
(Erase heading not required.)

Instructions regarding War Diaries and Intelligence Summaries are contained in F.S. Regs., Part II. and the Staff Manual respectively. Title pages will be prepared in manuscript.

Place	Date	Hour	Summary of Events and Information	Remarks and references to Appendices
SAILLY LA BOURSE	7/10/18	a.m.	16th Divl Headquarters moved from DROUVIN to SAILLY LA BOURSE.	
"	8/10/18	a.m.	Inspected the horses & mules & transport lines in advance'd detachment of 16th Divl R.F.A.	
"	"	p.m.	Inspected 145 Co. R.E.	
"	9/10/18	a.m.	Inspected 143 & 144 Co. R.E.	
"	10/10/18	"	Inspected the horses at 16th Divl Headquarters	
"	"	"	Inspected 47th Infy Bde transport	
"	11/10/18	"	Inspected horses & mules of Sylva Co.	
"	12/10/18	"	Attended Conference ADVS office Corps Headquarters	

Army Form C. 2118.

WAR DIARY
or
INTELLIGENCE SUMMARY.

(Erase heading not required.)

3

Place	Date	Hour	Summary of Events and Information	Remarks and references to Appendices
Sailly LaBourse	13/10/18	—	Inspected 111 to & 112 to Field Ambulance	
~	14/10/18	—	Inspected 113 to Field Ambulance	
~	15/10/18	—	Inspected 16 to Machine Gun Batt	
~	16/10/18	—	Inspected 16 DAC	
~	17/10/18	—	16 to Divl Head Quarters moved from Sailly LaBourse to Billy Berclau	
Billy Berclau	18/10/18	—	Inspected 112 to Field Ambulance 15th DDC. RE — Infantry — The Armoured Gus John Ban	
~	19/10/18	—	16 Divl Headquarters moved to PHALEMPIN	

Army Form C. 2118.

WAR DIARY
INTELLIGENCE SUMMARY

(4)

(Erase heading not required.)

Instructions regarding War Diaries and Intelligence Summaries are contained in F. S. Regs., Part II. and the Staff Manual respectively. Title pages will be prepared in manuscript.

Place	Date	Hour	Summary of Events and Information	Remarks and references to Appendices
PHALEMPIN	20/10/18		Inspected Batteries of 16th Divn. Headquarters	
"	21/10/18		16th Divl. Headquarters left Phalempin arrived Templeuve	
			Inspected 16th Divl. Train	
Templeuve	22/10/18			
"	23/10/18		Inspected 47th Divl. Headquarters	
"	24/10/18		Conference of V.O.s at D.D.V.S. Office	
			Inspected 47th Divl. A.T.c.	
"	25/10/18		Inspected 150th Bde R.F.A.	
"	26/10/18		Inspected Motor Amb. 1 16 Divl. Headquarters	
"	27/10/18		Inspected 4 9th Bdy. Buckinghams & 111th Batt.	
"	28/10/18		Inspected	

Army Form C. 2118.

WAR DIARY
or
INTELLIGENCE SUMMARY.
(Erase heading not required.)

Instructions regarding War Diaries and Intelligence Summaries are contained in F. S. Regs., Part II. and the Staff Manual respectively. Title pages will be prepared in manuscript.

Place	Date	Hour	Summary of Events and Information	Remarks and references to Appendices
TEMPLEUVE.	29/1/19		Inspected 45 Remounts arrived for the horse Examining 10 Cases of suspected poisoning at 22nd North'd Mobile Section.	
"	30/1/19.		DADVS made P.M. Examination on horse which died at the Hospital of 22nd North'd Mobile Section. Referred Corps Inspector poison to I Corps A.D.V.S.	
"	31/1/19.		Inspected the horses & mules of 158th Bde R.F.A. Inspected ob 47 MVS Inspected horses awaiting evacuation.	

Brennan D Vin
Major
DADVS 16th Division

WAR DIARY
or
INTELLIGENCE SUMMARY.
(Erase heading not required.)

Army Form C. 2118.

Place	Date	Hour	Summary of Events and Information	Remarks and references to Appendices
Templeuve	9-11-18		Inspected C.T.D. Rollers 177 & 73rd R.F.A.	
	10-11-18		16th Divl Headquarters moved from Templeuve to Taintignies	
Taintignies	11-11-18		Inspected No 1 Section 16 MG AT	
	12-11-18		Inspected Equipment of 2nd line A/C 5th & 6th Divisions. Inspected 46 Bty. B.E.A.(?) transport also 5th Royal Irish Lancers. 16 Sec. M.G. Rifles.	
	13-11-18		Inspected 47 Batty. B.E.A. Also transport and 16th held ? 14 Lancers and 9th Royal Highlanders	
	14-11-18		Inspected the transport B 49 LtT, Bde A/70 - 6th Armd Light Infy 24 Lancers and 18th Tanks	
	15-11-18		Inspected the transport B 10's & 157 Co's R.E.	
	16-11-18		Inspected the transport of 16th Machine Gun Batt. 16th Divl Headquarters moved to ATTICHES.	
ATTICHES	17-11-18		Inspected the horses & mules of A Batty. 169 Bde R.F.A.	

Army Form C. 2118.

WAR DIARY
INTELLIGENCE SUMMARY

(2)

(Erase heading not required.)

Instructions regarding War Diaries and Intelligence Summaries are contained in F. S. Regs., Part II. and the Staff Manual respectively. Title pages will be prepared in manuscript.

Place	Date	Hour	Summary of Events and Information	Remarks and references to Appendices
AVELIN	7/12/18		Inspected the horse lines of 180# Bde R.F.A.	
"	8/12/18		Inspects the transport 47th Infy Bde.	
"	9/12/18		Inspects 47th M.G.B. Vet. Section	
"	10/12/18		Inspects 6th Somerset L.I. & 34th London transport.	
"	11/12/18		Was in attended I Corps Races at Mouchin.	
"	12/12/18		Inspects B. Bnoos horse lines in 16th Brit. & Corps Committee	
"	13/12/18		Inspects the transport of 142 Co. 16 Instr. Train.	
"	14/12/18		Inspects the horse lines of 143, 144, 145 @ 16 Brit. Men	
"	15/12/18		Inspects the riding transport animals of 16 Bde H.Q.	
"	16/12/18		Inspects the transport of 22nd Hutts Inn. and 5th Royal Lich Regt	

Army Form C. 2118.

WAR DIARY
or
INTELLIGENCE SUMMARY.
(Erase heading not required.)

Instructions regarding War Diaries and Intelligence Summaries are contained in F. S. Regs., Part II. and the Staff Manual respectively. Title pages will be prepared in manuscript.

(3)

Place	Date	Hour	Summary of Events and Information	Remarks and references to Appendices
AVELIN	17/12/18		Inspected Tr: transport of 9th Royal Highlanders	
"	18/12/18		Inspected the transport of 112, 117, 113 Field Ambulances	
"	19/12/18		Inspected Mr transport of Machine Gun Batt. —	
"	20/12/18		Inspected the transport of 11th Tanks (P)	
"	21/12/18		Inspected 16th Divl Train transport	
"	22/12/18		Inspected 108th Bde R.F.A. — attached to 16th Divn.	
"	23/12/18		Inspects 75th Field Co. R.E. transport	
"	24/12/18		Inspects 16th Divl Headquarters transport transport	
"	25/12/18		Officer Class	
"	26/12/18		Davis attended 16th Divl Race Meeting	
"	27/12/18		Inspected the transport trains of Iolante Signal Co.	

Army Form C. 2118.

WAR DIARY
or
INTELLIGENCE SUMMARY.
(Erase heading not required.)

(4)

Instructions regarding War Diaries and Intelligence Summaries are contained in F.S. Regs., Part II. and the Staff Manual respectively. Title pages will be prepared in manuscript.

Place	Date	Hour	Summary of Events and Information	Remarks and references to Appendices
AVELIN	24/12/18		Inspected the transport of 16th Leinster Rifles, 2nd & 5th Royal Scots & 3rd Royal Scots.	
"	29/12/18		16th Div. Veterinary Board examined & classified the horses and mules of 16th Div. train.	
"	30/12/18		Board examined & classified the remount of 19th Royal Highlanders.	
"	31/12/18		Vety Board examined & classified the remount of 16th Leinster Rifle 22nd Northumberland Fus & 5th Royal Scots.	

Brennan de Vine
Major R.A.V.C.
D.A.D.V.S.
16th Division

1/1/19.

Army Form C. 2118.

9/3

WAR DIARY by DADVS
or
INTELLIGENCE SUMMARY. 16 Division

(Erase heading not required.)

Place	Date	Hour	Summary of Events and Information	Remarks and references to Appendices
AVELIN	1/1/19		Inspected th transport 7th & 18th Welch Regt - 47th Infy Bde. -	
"	2/1/19		Vety. Board visited 186th Bde R.F.A. & inspected classified all the horses & mules. The Bde. -	
"	3/1/19		Vety Board visited 106th Bde. A.F.A. attached 16th Division. Inspected & classified all the horses & mules to the Bde. -	
"	4/1/19		Veterinary Board inspected & classified all the horses & mules 3/166th Bde R.F.A. Headquarters & 4 & 6 Batys Bde 45 Bro.	
"	5/1/19		Vety Board inspected / classified all the horses, mules at 16 Divn H.Q.R.E. Hqrs & Trans 45 Bro.	

Army Form C. 2118.

WAR DIARY
or
INTELLIGENCE SUMMARY.
(Erase heading not required.)

(3)

Instructions regarding War Diaries and Intelligence Summaries are contained in F. S. Regs., Part II. and the Staff Manual respectively. Title pages will be prepared in manuscript.

Place	Date	Hour	Summary of Events and Information	Remarks and references to Appendices
AVELIN	13/1/19		Inspected horse lines of 108th Bde R.F.A.	
"	14/1/19		Met D.D.V.S. 3rd Army at 47th Mobile Vety Section - however I at Horse lines at PONT A MARCQ.	
"	15/1/19		Inspected with the Remount Demonstrator spare horses of the D.A.C. & 16th Mac Gun Bn. Inspected 185th Bde R.F.A. + 11th Tanks.	
"	16/1/19		Inspected the transport animals 1/157 C.Coy R.E. - R.E. H.Qrs. & Dum Ra.	
"	17/1/19		Inspection 6 mules of 117th Bde R.F.A.	
"	18/1/19		Inspected High Mobile Vety Section and received weekly statements	
"	19/1/19		Inspected 142 & 143 Coy A.S.C. 16 Div Train	
"	20/1/19		Inspected 3 horses for Sale at Pont a MARCQ	
"	21/1/19		Sale 1 Cart horse.	
"	22/1/19		Inspected the transport animals in stores at PONT A MARCQ	
"	23/1/19		Inspected the Transport animals of 156th & 155th Cos R.E.	

WAR DIARY
or
INTELLIGENCE SUMMARY.
(Erase heading not required.)

Army Form C. 2118.

by DADTS
16th Division

Place	Date	Hour	Summary of Events and Information	Remarks and references to Appendices
ANGLIN.	1/2/19		Inspected 105th A.F.A. Rgh. animals	
"	2/2/19		Routine.	
"	3/2/19		Inspected transport animals of 48th Inf. Bde.	
"	4/2/19		Inspected teams of 106th Divl. Train A.T.C.	
"	5/2/19		Attended sale of batchile horses from 24th Divisional at PONT A MARCQ.	
"	6/2/19		Capt. Cawthorn OC. 47 M.V.S. proceeded on 10 days leave to England. V. Corps Headquarters interviewed ADVS re sale of horses.	
"	7/2/19		Mallein horses at 16th Divl. Headquarters.	
"	8/2/19		Inspected the transport of 49th Inf. Bde.	
"	9/2/19		Inspected the transport of 47th Inf. Bde.	

WAR DIARY
or
INTELLIGENCE SUMMARY.
(Erase heading not required.)

Army Form C. 2118.

Place	Date	Hour	Summary of Events and Information	Remarks and references to Appendices
AVELIN	11/2/19		Inspected Mr. donkeys & mules 7/16 DAC.	
"	12/2/19		Attended Conference at Office PADVS I Corps	
"	13/2/19		Interviewed Mr Singer re Mar Q I arranged for sale between him & MARC Q —	
"	14/2/19		Conferred with ADVS examined horses for sale at DUNKIRQUE. —	
"	15/2/19		Inspected 10th Y animals from 16th DAC in lines sent to England. —	
"	16/2/19		Inspected the horses of MMP & 16th Div. also transport & animals of 111th & 112th to Sig. Co.	
"	17/2/19		Inspected the transport & animals of 152 & 157 & 75 RE	
"	18/2/19		Inspected the animals & transport of 156 & 155 RE	
"	19/2/19		Inspected the transport of 155 Co. RE.	

WAR DIARY
or
INTELLIGENCE SUMMARY

Army Form C. 2118.

Place	Date	Hour	Summary of Events and Information	Remarks and references to Appendices
AVELIN	20/2/19		Inspection with A.D.V.S. examined Horses for sale. Out AVELIN - 150 Animals issued.	
"	21/2/19		101 horses & mules sold by Public auction at Pont A Marcq. Horses in the main issued to Dutch Army I Corps	
"	22/2/19		Inspected the animals of 10th Me[dium] Jer[sey] Bat[tery]	
"	23/2/19		Cash Gisborne returning from leave in U.K. Inspected 177th Bde R.F.A.	
"	24/2/19		Inspected 160th Bde R.F.A.	
"	25/2/19		Return	
"	26/2/19		Instructed Capt Ray R.A.V.C. V.O. to 16 D.A.C. to proceed to Annual leaving. Capt Skrobyanne d later on V.V. for chg. V/M Court Morril Capt Nicholas to return for Annual leaving Capt ? 108 & 173 Bde to duty V.V.	

WAR DIARY
or
INTELLIGENCE SUMMARY.

Army Form C. 2118.

Place	Date	Hour	Summary of Events and Information	Remarks and references to Appendices
AVELIN	28/2/19		Others 10 to Bn: Parade at BERCES. Inspected Mr. Humm & men awaiting detail a transit at PONT A MARCQ. — Brennan Lt S the Major DADVS Lt Col Bn. 1/28/19